Grappling with God on the M25

A theology for everyday life

Frank Topping

Hodder & Stoughton

LONDON   SYDNEY   AUCKLAND

British Library Cataloguing in Publication Data
A record for this book is available from the British Library

ISBN 0 340 67851 8

Typeset by Avon Dataset Ltd, Bidford-on-Avon, Warks

Printed and bound in Great Britain by
Clays Ltd, St Ives plc

Hodder and Stoughton Ltd
A Division of Hodder Headline PLC
338 Euston Road
London NW1 3BH

Contents

Preface   v

1 Oh, God!
   Opening Soon: *An Impossible God*   1
   'Egg-head' Anselm and 'Clever-clogs' Aquinas *Existence
     of God 'proofs'*   12
2 Signs, Omens and Scientists
   Gesticulating Pyke *Astrology and fortune-telling*   20
   Agnostic Fish *Searching and questioning beliefs*   26
   Soundings *Spiritual language 'groans too deep for words'*   29
3 God's Truth
   It Ain't Necessarily So! *Bible 'truth' and history*   32
   Casting Stones *Interpreting and presenting 'facts'*   40
   The Kingdom of God is Like . . . *The 'upside-down' rule
     of love*   43
4 To Be a Pilgrim
   True Valour *The grateful pilgrim*   49
   Scallop, Staff and Scrip *'Pilgrimage' means 'moving on'*   54
   An English Joke   59
   A Cultural Revolution *A 'celestial' city – on earth?*   60
5 Perchance to Dream
   The Good Companions *The road to the Edinburgh
     Festival Fringe*   67
   Chad the Good Samaritan *The listening ministry*   70
   A Good Life Before Death *The hospice ministry*   74
   The Volunteers *The 'Here I am, send me' ministry*   78

The Styx: A Good Crossing *Death and bereavement*   81

A Good Lord on a Soapbox *Life after death*   91

Risen, But Not Yet Fully Ascended – Pardon? *Resurrection* 94

From the Ashes of Disaster *New beginnings –
  resurrection now (i)*   104

Start All Over Again *New beginnings – resurrection
  now (ii)*   107

6 Out! Out! Damned Spot!

Who, Me? *Guilt*   110

Forgiveness, Legally Speaking . . . *Forgiveness –
  God's and man's*   114

Veni, Vidi, Venues *Performance places and 'spaces'*   118

7 Out of the Depths, I Cry; Lord, Hear My Prayer

Doing Prayer *An approach to prayer*   121

Rendezvous *A family gathering*   125

Prescription Prayers and Crystal Castles *Meditation
  and contemplation*   127

Your Sea is so Large and My Barque so Small *Sailors,
  the sea and prayer*   136

8 In Deserts, Gardens and Kitchens

Burning Sands and Cool, Clear Water *Being alone with
  your thoughts*   140

'Oh, God, You Are Clever!' *'I'll praise my maker
  while I've breath'*   145

Lord of the Pots and Pans *The practice of the presence
  of God*   149

9 Agonising in Body, Mind and Spirit

'My God, My God, Why Have You Forsaken Me?'
  Thinking about suffering   153

Pulpits, Fonts and Communion Tables *Sacraments:
  Baptism and Eucharist*   171

Bagpipe, Kilt and Sporran   179

Preface

Most of the 'grappling' in this book occurred during conversations that took place while travelling around the United Kingdom doing theatrical things in churches and theatres and religious things in radio and television studios. The conversations, about God, the World, the Meaning of Life, and several other related issues, were between me and my wife, June, and a motley selection of the great, the good, and the not so good.

Although these exchanges were fairly accurately recorded, the sequence in which they occurred is of no particular significance. As Eric Morecambe once famously said to André Previn, (or was it Andrew Preview?), 'All the right notes are there, Sunshine, but not necessarily in the right order.'

This is, largely, a theological book, but it is neither 'systematic' nor comprehensive. It might have been called, *Topping's Unsystematic* which has a certain appeal because theology does not happen to one 'systematically'. People ask the most searching questions without warning: 'Is there life after Death? Do you believe I will see my mother again?' Clearly, it would not be appropriate to reply to such questions by saying, 'Before I answer that, perhaps we should consider first some of the classical arguments for the existence of God.' There is nothing for it; you have to 'grapple' like 'Wrestling Jacob' with questions as and when they are put to you.

The concept of 'grappling' stems from an experience I

once had in a small boat with our sons Simon and Mark, when we had found ourselves held fast to the seabed as if something supernatural had clasped hold of the anchor and was steadfastly refusing to release it, no matter how much we heaved at the anchor warp. With a rising tide and a gale warning, our anxiety levels were reaching new and hitherto unexperienced heights. I knew I could always cut the anchor free, but that would mean losing our best anchor.

I started the engine and drove back and forth over the anchor. It remained immovable. Perhaps foolishly, I tried to search the seabed using another small anchor as a grappling hook in a vain attempt to discover what was holding the anchor. Many strange objects emerged from the depths – fascinating, but not particularly helpful. Eventually, our combined efforts succeeded in raising the anchor above the water and into sight. Amazingly, an anchor fluke had hooked into a metal ring which was attached to the seabed by two lengths of heavy chain. Releasing the fluke from the ring involved a considerable amount of effort and ingenuity, especially as the grappling hook had also become entangled with the chain. Grappling with God, I feel, requires no less exertion, mentally, spiritually, or emotionally.

Once, in the Mediterranean, June and I listened to a drama unfolding over our little ship's VHF radio, as some poor soul called for help while 'grappling' with a fast-held anchor. In the end he had cut the warp and abandoned his anchor, leaving the mystery of its fastness on the bottom of the sea. Sometimes you have to do that, perhaps especially when you are 'grappling' with God.

Frank Topping
London 1998

1 Oh, God!

Opening Soon: *An Impossible God*

I was in the inside lane and signalled my intention to come off the roundabout at the next exit. I hesitated because of the white van. The driver of the van, who sported a back-to-front baseball cap and who had, for several miles, been driving so close as to make me suspect that he might just possibly have caught his bumper on my tow-bar, was now accompanying me on the outside lane of the roundabout. We had passed three of the roundabout's exits and he was still keeping level with no apparent intention of turning off, which he didn't.

'Oh, God!' I said, standing on the brakes as he drove straight across my bows. As he passed, a tattooed right arm made a dramatic movement out of the driver's window.

'What does he think he's doing?' asked my wife, as her head tunnelled into the passenger-seat head-rest and road maps, mobile phone and a bag of tomatoes shot off her lap.

'Making a gesture, I think, though I doubt it was liturgical.'

We were on the A2, not very far from Canterbury, and a thought crossed my mind.

'Ha!' I said. 'Did you know that St Augustine very nearly didn't come to England because of the reports he was given about the local inhabitants being wild, unruly and uncivilised? It's just as well he didn't come up the A2. He'd have been back on the ferry before you could say, '*Dominus*

Vobiscum'. Terrified he was. He went all the way back to Rome to ask Gregory the Great if he was absolutely certain that he was the right man for the job. Funny, isn't it, how the people who least want to do a particular job frequently seem to end up doing it.'

'Keep your eyes open for the Chartham Hatch sign,' June said. 'You have to go off to the left first, remember? Yes, here it is. We get on to the other side of the A2 and drive back in the opposite direction.'

'Rather a complicated way of turning right. No wonder Augustine decided to stay in Canterbury.'

We turned off for Chartham Hatch and June said, 'Assuming that God had something to do with the choosing of Augustine, and assuming God exists, why do people also assume that God is male?'

'Patriarchal arrogance and ignorance, I suppose.'

'Oh, look! It's a hawk!'

'Where?'

'There, sitting on that post!'

The lane was heavy with summer green. Trees attempted to reach from one side of the road to the other. High up they succeeded. In hedge gaps there were glimpses of red bricked oast houses, like giant white-capped cockerels, standing guard over acres of hop poles.

Not long after we passed the village hall, June said, 'Mark you, I suppose whether or not God exists is probably somewhat more important than God's gender really, isn't it?'

We were now at the gates of the house. 'Shall we pursue this before tea, or after?'

'After.'

'Right.'

We had found the music for our first touring production here, in this house, with its sweeping drive and classically pillared front door. Sitting around the fire basket, where not one but two fireplaces had been removed before the original had been found, Maurice Copus had listened to our plans for the adaptation of my book on the Passion, *An Impossible God*, into a play for one actor. Could it be done? Could one actor perform a Passion-play?

The germ of the idea had begun its life in Belfast where I had been asked to read extracts from *An Impossible God* in a series of Holy Week services of reconciliation between Catholics and Protestants. It was an inspired and prophetic idea to have a series of services of reconciliation throughout Holy Week. After all, where else could reconciliation be found, if not in the Passion? A dozen or more years later, in 1998, there was poignant significance in the fact that the 'Agreement' was signed on a Good Friday.

In my mind's eye I can still see the packed churches, still recall my surprise at the almost crackling intensity of the audience, hear the acute silence, as characters from the Passion narrative sprang to life, became real people, agonising and arguing about good and evil, suffering, death and resurrection. I should not have been surprised. I should have realised that suffering, death and resurrection were not academic subjects in Northern Ireland.

About a week earlier, in England, I had completed a riotous tour of a one-man play about the American novelist, John Steinbeck. I had never attempted a full length one-man performance before. When the 'Snap' People's Theatre Company had invited me to play an American re-enacting stories involving a range of American dialects, it wasn't just the dialects that concerned me, but whether or not I possessed the pzazz, oomph or stamina to stand, sit, strut, sing, shout, laugh, weep and rivet an audience to their seats for that length of time.

I had performed in a two-man show, in the West End with Donald Swann, but a one-man show was another question altogether. The very idea of a one-man play suggests an isolated pilgrimage, a public baring of the soul, or at least so I thought until I started doing it. It quickly became clear to me that the exercise involved stepping on to a stage not alone but accompanied by a whole army of intimately known companions; a company of veterans who had a history of shared adventures, comic and tragic disasters and who now met night after night, like old friends to relive what was probably the most exciting and terrifying period of their lives.

The tour of Steinbeck's *Once there was a War* took us to small towns, theatres, schools, village halls, studio theatres, public libraries, town halls and art centres. During the tour, industrial action was being taken by a teachers' union which involved a ban on overtime. As a result we performed in lots of schools, mainly because it meant the whole school could be marched into the assembly hall and kept occupied for an afternoon with a minimal requirement of teaching staff.

One of the basic lessons learned during that period was that when performing to an entire school you should never indulge in a dramatic pause that lasts much longer than a second, because if you do, the school scallywag will undoubtedly fill your pause with what might best be described as 'unsuitable', if not downright vulgar, sound effects. Yet even in these circumstances, the magic and the drama won through, achieving a variety of reactions from stunned silences to spontaneous outbursts of applause, which was particularly satisfying if the performance had begun in an atmosphere which contained an element of belligerent, bubble-gum-chewing, arms-folded animosity.

One particular booking, inexplicably, was in a youth club in Hertfordshire. I don't know how the booking had come about, but it obviously had not been advertised to the club members. Perhaps it had been meant as a surprise. It certainly proved to be a surprise for a number of the regulars.

The performance space was a kind of pit at one end of a room, with a semi-circular rail around its edge. The pit, under normal circumstances, must have housed a table-tennis table, because during the first twenty minutes or so of the performance late-arriving youths were heard to complain,

'What's happen to the table-tennis, then?' (the space being filled with our portable set which included a huge, tank-camouflage net – and me).

Some of the audience sat in the semi-circular seating above the pit, some leaned on the rail smoking, and one particularly offensive young man threw his dog-ends into the pit itself. Initially, the feeling of hostility was so great that I almost despaired. At one point, during the first few minutes, I wondered whether it might be best to admit defeat and pack up. However, I was very aware that people other than me, like our stage manager, Jonathan Cann, were dependent on the performance being completed and the fee paid, so I battled on.

Because of the lighting I could not actually see much of the audience, but I could hear them laughing and talking among themselves. An unconscious pattern of performance began to emerge. Whenever I heard someone talk, instinctively, I would move towards them and perform in that direction as loudly as I could. I performed jokes as broadly as possible, I exaggerated gestures and movements, and not always inappropriately; parts of this play did demand larger-than-life performance. Eventually, I needed only to turn my head in a particular direction to achieve silence. I don't know how long it took, but eventually I was aware that the entire audience had tuned in and were being held by the drama of Steinbeck's story. An hour and a half suddenly passed and to my amazement the end of the performance was greeted by tumultuous applause. Perhaps the most satisfying moment came as I was leaving, when I was stopped at the door by a young man who said, 'You're all right, mate – for a Yank.'

Such adrenaline-creating challenges were memorable and exciting but, of course, the most magical and enjoyable experiences occurred when the play was presented to people who came with enthusiastic expectation, people who willingly and joyfully entered into the adventure of the play. Under these circumstances the location of the performance space is secondary; it doesn't matter if it is a church hall or a fully equipped theatre.

Schools and the youth club, unsympathetic audiences or even a positively hostile audience had taught me valuable lessons, but it was the people who understood the conventions, picked up undertones, overtones and nuances who enabled us to realise the full potential of Steinbeck's magic. These were the people who eventually convinced me of what I had set out to discover, that the one-man play was within my compass.

It is a truism, of course, that the one-man performance is never achieved by one person; in a sense there is no such thing as a one-man play. There are so many other elements that contribute to bringing it off. 'Alchemy' is the word that springs to mind – a combination of skills, stage management and lighting that, at its best, creates magic, mystery and miracle.

The casting of the storyteller's spell involves the active participation and involvement of the audience, a willing suspension of disbelief, a desire to enter into the make-believe world that is being summoned – not out of thin air but out of shared common human experience, shared knowledge of laughter and grief.

The readers of a novel will know, or will sense, that the depth of a good author's knowledge of their characters is far greater and much more detailed than they are prepared or are able to share in the book. An audience will also be aware that the storyteller's words, and the actor's delivery of them, are merely iceberg tips, the light-catching undulating peaks of a submerged mountain of experience. For instance, the story of the Passion of Jesus Christ strikes deep universal chords, but the fact that the version of the story told in *An Impossible God* was written at a time when my own life prognosis was in serious question no doubt contributed one of the subconscious layers that perhaps gives an unspoken authority and authenticity to the book.

The dust of the Steinbeck tour had not quite settled before I found myself standing in a packed church, in Belfast. I was reading a passage about betrayal and violence and death in another, not dissimilar, city, two thousand years earlier, then occupied and controlled by a military force, in a society riven with religious and political sects and divisions. In such a situation the atmosphere could hardly have been other than it was – electric.

I had written *An Impossible God* as a devotional exercise, a study of the death and resurrection stories of Jesus Christ linked to the Stations of the Cross, which is a religious practice that emerged from the medieval church. I had not conceived it as a play or even thought of it as containing 'performance' pieces, but standing in that pulpit in Belfast, its dramatic potential leaped off the page, demanding an actor's interpretation.

The Stations of the Cross is a very ancient form of devotion practised throughout the year, but it has special significance in Lent and Holy Week. There is evidence from a very early date that Christian pilgrims to Jerusalem made a practise of following the traditional route taken by Jesus from the house of the Roman Governor, Pontius Pilate, to Calvary and ultimately to the tomb in which Jesus was laid. As they made this journey they would stop and recall particular incidents in the Passion at various places along the route and pray and meditate on the sufferings of Christ.

Modern pilgrims find the stations marked, carved in stone tablets, along the Via Dolorosa in the Suk, the Arab market in the old city which hardly seems to have changed its atmosphere since biblical times. In Jerusalem, every day of every week but particularly in the days of Holy Week, hundreds of pilgrims walk in the steps of Jesus, praying at each of the Stations of the Cross. At each station the pilgrim, in devotional imagination, relives the event associated with the place, sees the crowds, hears the shouts of traders, and attempts to feel the emotional involvement of those who were

first touched by the terrible drama of Christ's Passion. For
example, in *An Impossible God*, the story of the meeting
between Jesus and Mary, his mother, is recaptured as if we
were witnessing the original event.

The Fourth Station: Jesus Meets His Mother

> *Mary did not speak,*
> *did not weep,*
> *did not touch,*
> *but they met.*
>
> *In the lane*
> *from the Damascus Gate*
> *dealers touted for custom,*
> *money-changers eyed travellers,*
> *assessing their worth, wary.*
> *The air,*
> *thick with aromas,*
> *spices, meat on spits,*
> *animals and people,*
> *and noise,*
> *hooves and hammers*
> *clanking, clinking,*
> *clucking, bleating,*
> *soldiers joking,*
> *women, children,*
> *shouting, laughing.*
>
> *In the midst of babble,*
> *they met,*
> *in a pocket*
> *of love-charged silence.*
>
> *All her life*
> *she had searched for him,*

the child she had held
but could not hold,
the elusive core of him
beyond her reach.
But now,
in one long look
the years compressed,
from cradle to Egypt,
from carpentry
to Hosannas on a donkey,
Simeon's sword sinking deeper,
and yet,
she was nearer to him now
than she had ever been.

The mystery of his birth,
the mystery of his being
touched her, embraced her
into the mystery of his death.

When tears came
they did not reproach,
neither was there question
in her pain;
but in the din
of money and men,
alone with him,
her silence said,
'Behold, the handmaid of the Lord.'

In Canterbury, Maurice Copus had created a theatre company that specialised in producing plays that were suitable for performance in churches and cathedrals. They had performed T. S. Eliot's *Murder in the Cathedral* in the crypt of Canterbury Cathedral, and plays like Robert Bolt's *A Man for All Seasons*, and Christopher Fry's *The Firstborn* and *Boy with a Cart*, and Dorothy L. Sayers, *The Zeal of Thy House*. June and I had known Maurice for years, so not unnaturally we went to him when the idea of presenting *An Impossible God* as a play began to emerge.

The current production of *An Impossible God* involves an element of son et lumière, in that each scene and character is isolated by minimal atmospheric lighting, and each speech reaches its conclusion accompanied by a piece of music. The lights fade and the last reverberations of the music linger in the air before the next scene and character appears in another area. Scenes elide one into the other. It's a kind of theatrical sleight of hand. Costumes are suggested by a range of different coloured clothes, a cloak and one or two props. The simplicity of the staging and the lighting of the performance means that it can be performed almost anywhere, but perhaps the stone columns of an English country church provide the best and most natural setting for a Passion-play.

They say that one of the ways of surviving is to re-invent yourself every ten years. After a reasonably successful decade as a broadcaster, writer and performer, a number of events, culminating in an illness, brought my progress to a sudden standstill. I was out of circulation long enough for the rumours of my demise to be interpreted, in certain circles, as truth. I needed to put myself back on the map. I needed to wave a large flag announcing the fact that not only had I survived but I was alive and well and kicking. We had a council of war and decided that what we needed was a showcase.

Knowing now that the one-man show was something I could handle, we considered the possibility of taking a play to the Edinburgh Festival Fringe. However, it did not take much research to discover that one-man plays were not exactly a rarity at the Fringe. In fact, it is as easy to sink without trace at the Edinburgh Fringe as anywhere else, probably easier. At that time, Fringe events programmes revealed that somewhere in the region of a thousand shows were looking for an audience on the opening night of the festival. You did not need to be a great mathematician to calculate that the average audience would be exceedingly small in number. By the end of the first week many companies despair, pack up and leave town. Most companies lose money. To break even would indicate an unusual degree of success. To be able to announce a profit would be tantamount to a runaway success.

An essential ingredient for any degree of success was a review in the *Scotsman*, preferably a good one, or at least one with a good quote in it. One thousand shows also informed the reasonably astute publicist that no matter how valiant the efforts of the *Scotsman*, there would not be enough reviewers to go around. Clearly the *Scotsman* would have to make its own short list. So, what to do?

If one-man shows had lost their rarity value, what else could be done that might possibly raise one's profile enough to be noticed by the various reviewers in national and local radio and television and in the press?

Gradually the idea began to emerge of creating a perform-ance marathon, in the form of *three* one-man plays, per-formed by one actor. Almost regardless of the quality of the productions, the marathon element alone might attract attention. Three full-length plays performed successively by one person would involve no less than four and half hours of memorised texts. Attracting attention is a necessary element in the game, but having got people's attention, winning their approval by the quality of both production and performance is also an essential ingredient for longer-term survival.

The performances and productions would have to be honed, revised and tested on the road and before many audiences before the opening night in Edinburgh. We could not try things out in Edinburgh, or plan to 'get it right by the end of the Festival'. To have any hope of success, each production needed to be professional, powerful, and breath-taking from the word 'Go!'

The three shows would be very different from each other. They would consist of:

1. *Laughing in my Sleep* – A revue performance not unlike the two-man show with Donald Swann but with lots of newly written or produced sketches and pieces.
2. A Passion-play based on *An Impossible God*.
3. The John Steinbeck play, now entitled *The Steinbeck Dispatches*.

I don't think we had any idea of what we were really committing ourselves to, but it was to open up a whole new way of life.

We spent yet another extraordinarily pleasant evening at Chartham Hatch, eating, reminiscing, discussing the one-man three plays' venture, remembering plays and players, talking about books and people, singing songs at the piano and laughing a lot. A good night, revelling in each other's company, warmed by friendship. Just what we needed, therapeutic, refreshing, a tonic.

'Egg-head' Anselm and 'Clever-clogs' Aquinas

We were back on the road, the comforts and delights of Chartham Hatch and Canterbury behind us. Ahead of us lay Dunstable and a performance in the Methodist church in the Square. Approaching Dunstable from Kent, the almost unavoidable M25 lies before the traveller heading north-west. It doesn't matter really which way you go from this direction; if you go to the west or to the east, it's about the same distance either way round. You could, of course, choose to cross London, but there's never much of a lull in London traffic, apart from very late at night or perhaps extremely early in the morning. London is always buzzing with life and cars, at almost any hour of the day, and then there are traffic lights, diversions and one-way systems. So you end up opting for east or west around London's encircling motorway.

We joined the M25 at Sevenoaks and settled down in the slow lane. I suppose we have a kind of philosophy now about motorway driving, having driven close to a quarter of a million miles in the last several years, taking our plays to various places. Inevitably, you develop a survival philosophy. Our philosophy is based on the observation that in the United Kingdom roads seem to have their own speed. If you drive for a period of two or three hours up, down or across almost any stretch of the British road system, it doesn't much matter if you drive fast and neurotically, or as calmly and as moderately as you can; the difference in time at the end is hardly worth the effort expended. There will, however, be a big difference in how you feel. If you drive very fast, you will inevitably arrive at your destination tense, muscles aching, close to exhaustion, and feeling you've done a hard day's work. If, on the other hand, you choose the slow lane, and drive at about sixty, having conversations, listening to the radio and eating the occasional apple, you don't feel so tense or so wound up, and you don't arrive all that much later than your fast-driving counterpart.

On motorways, in heavy traffic, we've found that it doesn't matter which lane you are in. You seem to keep more or less level with the same vehicles whether you are in the slow, middle or fast lane. You keep seeing that vehicle from Pocklington in Yorkshire, the green one, with 'wash me' written in the dust on the back. The difference is your physical and mental condition at the end of the drive. In the slow lane you feel relaxed, in the fast you don't. It's as simple as that.

We pulled on to the infamous M25 and settled down to enjoy life in the slow lane. 'Life in the Slow Lane' sounds like a good title for a book.

June said, 'The existence of God, we didn't really get on

to that, did we? Can the existence of God be proved?'

'I think the short answer to that is, "No". I suppose if you could *prove* the existence of God there wouldn't be anybody in the world who wouldn't believe in God and there would be no need for faith, would there? If God was provable, if you could draw up an equation that said, 'A+B = God', if it was as simple as that, then you certainly wouldn't need faith. There's another interesting word, 'faith'. What does it mean?

'Anselm, saint, scholar and sometime Archbishop of Canterbury, thought of faith as being part of a rational process. He thought that the creeds and the statements of belief about God were always consistent with rationality. His great theme was "*fides quaerens intellectum*" – faith seeking intelligent explanation. On the other hand, someone like Martin Luther would say faith isn't to do with the intellectual acceptance of a set of creeds. "Faith", he said, "is a personal thing. Faith concerns trust, faith unites the believer to God." In other words, for Martin Luther, to have faith was to live as God intended us to live. For Martin Luther, faith wasn't just an intellectual exercise; it was to do with personal experience, a personal relationship with God. That was what John Wesley discovered when he eventually came to faith. He said, "I felt my heart strangely warmed, I felt that I did trust in Christ . . . that he had taken away *my* sins . . . even *mine*." For Wesley, faith became a personal experience.'

'Hang on,' said June. 'We've got on to faith. I thought we were supposed to be talking about the existence of God.'

'You're absolutely right,' I said. 'Let's get back to Anselm and his intellectual approach to proving the existence of God. Now you're not going to like this, but there is no way round it. I don't know any other word for this argument other than the one that the text-books use. I'm afraid dear old Anselm gave the world a theory that is known in theological circles as the "ontological" argument. If I have understood it properly, a condensed version of it might put the argument like this: if you can conceive the existence of something than which nothing greater nor anything more perfect exists or can be conceived – and it is possible to conceive something than which nothing greater exists – then whatever that is, is God.

'Neat, isn't it? But it is a flawed argument. After all, just because you can conceive of something doesn't mean it has to exist, does it? Nevertheless, Anselm's argument has fascinated philosophers for centuries and thinkers keep revisiting the idea and examining it. Now Anselm was an eleventh-century man, but if you think he was a bit tasty in the logical and sophistry department, just wait until you get to the thirteenth century where you meet up with an absolute clever-clogs in the form of Thomas Aquinas. He came up with no less than five ways of "proving" the existence of God.

'The first is the "prime-mover" theory. The idea is that everything is moving, the world is not static. Snow and rain fall from the sky, springs spring up, streams run, rocks tumble down hillsides. But why? Why is nature in motion? Why is nature not still? Aquinas argued that nothing moves of its own accord, everything that moves has something which started it moving. If you keep going back to the thing that moved the thing, that moved the thing, you eventually get back to the "prime-mover", the cause of all this movement. The "prime-mover", he argues, must be the source of all movement, that is God.'

'Judging by the lights up ahead,' June said, 'it looks as if the "prime-mover" is about to stop all movement on the M25. I don't know what it is, but we are all slowing down.'

One of the great mysteries of motorways is why the traffic suddenly slows down and then starts moving again and stops again. It could be a whole variety of things, of course. If it's road-works you usually get a sign, an advance warning, indicating that you are going to come across several miles of cones. There will be no actual sign of any work going on behind the cones, but several miles of cones will slow down the traffic. It could be that something has happened on the other side of the motorway and people are 'rubber-necking'; it could be that there has been an accident miles ahead of you. The frustrating thing is that usually you can't do anything about it. The traffic slows down and sometimes comes to a stop as it did now. Then June spotted them in the rear-view mirror.

'Here they come,' she said. 'Blue lights dashing up the hard shoulder. There must have been an accident.' She threw a sweater from her lap over her shoulder to land on a box of sound cables behind us. 'So, Aquinas and the "prime-mover", that's the first argument. What's the second one?'

I laughed, 'Curiously enough, we could use this motorway situation as an example of his second argument, as it's very similar to the "prime-mover" argument. It's called the "first cause" argument. It argues that every event is caused by something and if you keep going back to the first cause, then the first cause will be God.'

'So God's the cause of this hold-up on the motorway?'

'Well, ultimately, I suppose you have to say "yes".'

'OK, what about his third argument?'

'The third argument is the "cosmological" argument. They do summon up some wonderful words, these arguments. In the cosmological argument he says that the fact that we exist requires an explanation. Everything points beyond itself to other things. For example, the existence of this motorcar is dependent on a whole range of other things; factory workers, sheets of metal, wood from the Scandinavian forests, rubber from gum trees. The world depends on the sun, the sun on its place in the universe and so on. But if in time you reached something that was not dependent on anything, and eventually you would have to reach that point, then that independent thing would have to be God. The flaw in that argument would be the question: Why would you have to reach a point when there was an absolutely independent something? Perhaps everything is, quite simply, dependent on something else.'

We were trickling along now in that desultory way, so familiar to M25-drivers. You move a few yards, stop, move another few yards, stop again.

'Look,' said June. 'There's a service station, Clacket Lane, up ahead. Why don't we pull off and have a cup of tea? With any luck by the time we come back on the motorway this will have cleared itself up.'

'Good idea,' I said.

On we trickled, forward, stop, forward, stop. About ten minutes later we pulled off the motorway and into the service station. We made our way past the games area where lots of people were pretending to be driving vehicles on a motorway, you could hear the noise of the screeching brakes and the horns. It always puzzles me why people who have just come off a motorway should play a game where they are pretending to be on a motorway. But there, human nature is a very mysterious thing.

We sat down with our tea.

'So then, where were we? The fourth argument, wasn't it?'

'Oh, yes. Aquinas's five arguments for the existence of God. His fourth argument is about human values such as truth, goodness, integrity, nobility, the appreciation of enjoyment and beauty. Where do these values come from? Aquinas argues that there must be something that is, in itself, true, good and noble. Ultimate goodness, therefore, he argued, is God.

'The fifth argument, which is probably the most popular of all the arguments, again has one of those tediously long names. It's called the "teleological" argument. It's an argument which seems to have a universal appeal. It was put into a relatively modern idiom in the eighteenth century by a man called William Paley. His explanation of Aquinas's fifth theory is known as "Paley's watch". Probably a bit easier to remember, as a title, than Aquinas's "teleological" argument.

'Paley's watch analogy puts the argument into a nutshell.

He said that if you were walking in a desert place and saw a rock lying on the ground and you asked yourself, "How did that rock come to exist?" it would be quite reasonable for you to put its existence down to chance – the chance result of the action of natural forces, such as wind and rain, heat and cold. So, you might reason, after a few thousand years of weathering a crack appeared in a big lump of rock and a smaller piece fell off, and that is the rock that is lying in front of you. But if you saw a watch lying on the ground you would not argue that this complex instrument had just "happened", that the cogs and springs, wheels, axles and balances had accidentally come together to form a function-ing machine. That would be absolutely implausible. We would be obliged to admit to the existence of an intelligent, creative mind, a watchmaker, a designer. Paley then pointed out that the world in which we live is extremely complex, the human brain is complex, the solar system and the universe comprise a far more complex creation than the most sophisti-cated of watches. Therefore it is reasonable to suppose that there is an intelligent, creative mind at the nub of the universe and that mind is God.

'None of these arguments are watertight "proofs" of the existence of God, but I think they do suggest, quite persua-sively, that it is not unreasonable to suppose that there might well be, at the heart of all creation, an intelligent, thinking, reasoning mind that embraces such things as truth and goodness.'

We finished our tea and left the restaurant. As we passed the shop, June said, 'Shall we get a newspaper?'

'Good idea,' I said. 'It will help pass the time until the next set of cones.'

'Well, it will help pass the time for me,' she said, 'because it's your turn to drive.'

The traffic seemed to be flowing again as we got back on to the M25 and June said, 'Of course, most people who believe in God don't know anything about these peculiar arguments of Aquinas or St Anselm, and on the whole I doubt if they would want to know. But there must be some kind of logic behind most people's belief in God, even if it's not nicely reasoned, wouldn't you say?'

'Yes, I think you're right, and it's probably based on "experience" rather than reason. One of the most difficult things to argue with is people's perceived experience of God. Once you've had a religious "experience", argument becomes redundant. After all, you can say, with considerable authority, "I don't have to believe in the existence of my wife, because I *know* her." In the same way, I do not have to believe in the existence of God, because I *know* God.

'A great thinker in the field of psychoanalysis, Carl Gustav Jung, a world-renowned psychiatrist who practised in Zurich, believed that an awareness of the spiritual, religious dimension to life was at the heart of health. Sigmund Freud, on the other hand, believed that religion was a neurotic excuse for not coping with life. People invented religion in order to comfort themselves. Jung found, on the contrary, that in his experience people functioned better when they had a spiritual understanding of life. He thought that a belief in God was natural and that not believing in God was unnatural. He once said, "Among all my patients in the second half of life, that is to say, over thirty-five, there hasn't been one whose problem in the last resort didn't turn out to be a need to find a religious outlook on life." He said, "It's safe to say that every one of them fell ill because they had lost that which the living religions of every age had given to their followers, and none of them had been healed who didn't regain their religious outlook." In a television interview, a few months before Jung died, he was asked if he believed in God. And he replied, "No, I do not *believe* in God . . . I *know* God".'

2 Signs, Omens and Scientists

Gesticulating Pyke

In between the journeys, setting up the sound systems, rigging up the lights and giving performances, my broadcasting continues, the most consistent outlet being Terry Wogan's BBC Radio 2 programme. I've been popping up on Terry's breakfast show now for something over twenty-five years and, depending on where we might be performing our shows, I will either go into his studio in Broadcasting House or do it 'down a line' from an unattended studio. The BBC has unattended studios all over the country and in some of the unlikeliest places, such as rooms in town halls and public libraries or, as I remember in one case, a room down a back alley where I had to get the key from the local police station. On the other hand, you might have the good fortune to be in an 'unattended' studio in a local radio station, where at least you have the comfort of BBC staff to help you if you get into difficulties.

On one occasion, the unattended studio where I should have been broadcasting from had actually 'gone down', that is ceased to function, at the critical moment for some mysterious reason. I found myself marching in to someone's office and asking if I could use their telephone. I called the familiar number in London and while I was being patched through to the studio, the person whose office it was began to suggest that it might be more convenient if I looked for a phone somewhere else. At that moment I heard Terry

Wogan's voice in the earpiece, clearly about to bring me into his programme. I addressed the person concerned in the kind of voice usually associated only with the SAS, a voice that brooked no argument. Suddenly, I found myself alone in the office, and heard Terry Wogan saying, 'That's my boy, Frank Topping, coming through – through thick and thin!' Whether or not my SAS voice was heard on the air, I was never quite sure. Terry was well aware that I was not in a studio, and he greeted me by saying, 'You sound as if you've got a bucket on your head.' However, at least I had got through, and was broadcasting, even if it was with a bucket on my head.

On one happy occasion I was able to combine going to Terry's studio in Broadcasting House and then nipping round to Hammersmith, to the home of Dr Magnus Pyke. Magnus was a very well-known television broadcaster on scientific subjects and famous for the extraordinary gyrations he went through, the amazing way in which he used his arms and hands when he was explaining some scientific theory. It was almost as if his arms and hands did not belong to him, but were being manipulated by a trainee puppeteer who had not quite got the hang of it yet.

In this meeting we were united – scientist and Christian – in a mutual impatience with astrology, fortune-telling, signs and omens. I began by asking, 'Magnus, what would your objections be to astrology and fortune-telling?'

Both of his hands described a variety of arcs and circles before coming to rest on either side of his face. 'My main objection,' his left hand attempted flight but he snapped it back, 'would be – that it is not true, it's false.' He crossed his legs, twice. 'How can a hack working for the *Daily Mirror*, writing on what the stars foretell, know whether it is a good day for me to indulge in broadcasting, or investing my money, or whatever? It's all rubbish!' Both arms became activated; they were neither emphasising nor gesticulating, they were just activated.

'It started way, way back when people were suffering the uncontrolled trials and tribulations of a savage world. Seeing the stars and moon unaffected in their courses people thought therefore it would be nice if constellations had something to do with real life. It wasn't so then, it isn't so now. It's nonsense. We have so much of this nonsense. This superstition is a corrosive force in our society. Take dowsing, water-divining.' His arms became tree branches at the mercy of an unseen but clearly very strong wind.

'They go round with a little twig. There have been a number of tests where they have had running water under-neath. It's pure nonsense! It comes from the old days of fortune-telling, when you took a bundle of twigs, threw them over your shoulder and the way they fell gave you some idea as to what was going on. You could equally well take the intestines of a cow and throw them over your shoulder. It's the same sort of thing.' His left arm scratched his right ear from behind his head.

'Do you know that in America now there are a tremendous number of people who *seriously* believe in UFOs? Little men with electric lights sticking out of their heads! They believe that the Pentagon has captured a number of these and are keeping them secret. It's called "Cosmic Watergate"! This is the kind of trouble that getting wrapped up in this nonsense can get you into!' His arms folded briefly but the right hand was clearly about to begin further explorations of the ether.

I was sitting at quite a safe distance so I said, 'Some people do take astrology very seriously. I know a number of people who turn to their stars as the first thing in the paper.'

His left arm shot out, his forefinger stabbing the air. 'And if their stars tell them, "You are the master race, go out and slaughter all the Jews, or all the black people, or whoever", this is the sort of danger that they get into! Look at all these bogus religions, where they all go into South America.' The arms outlined most of the southern hemisphere. 'And drink prussic acid!' The hands were now compulsively sketching

Antarctica. 'This is the sort of danger that belief in this kind of thing can involve. And I think it's very menacing.' The left elbow trapped the right hand beneath the left armpit.

I dragged my eyes away from the undulating limbs and said, 'Astrologers present arguments suggesting that the heavenly bodies affect the earth and therefore affect us. Is that in any way true?'

'No evidence!' Both hands grasped the underside of his chair as if expecting it to make a dash for it. 'I looked all this up knowing I was going to be discussing this with you. There are signs of the zodiac where – you are going to be a master.' Convulsive hand to the right. 'And if you were born under *other* signs of the zodiac – you were going to be a servant!' Left hand out, right hand to the back of the head. 'Supposing your parents said, "I want you to be a Leo, or a Virgo or whatever it is". By inducing your birth you can change your star, it's as silly as that. These things are, I think, very menacing and dangerous.' He began to conduct the *New World Symphony*. 'The Mars effect! Somebody had the great new idea that if you were born when Mars was in a certain constellation you'd be a great athlete. And they took all these Sebastian Coes, all these great athletes out, and when they went into it, there was absolutely nothing in it at all!' The arms had finished the first, or quite possibly the second, movement.

'Levitation was the latest. You can go to New Zealand and pay about 2,500 dollars after you've done your transcendental meditation so that you can rise two or three feet and hang there! And people believed this, and paid all this money! What you did was, you started with a specially expensive lesson – hopping!' Both hands became kangaroos, hopping alternately. 'To believe this nonsense may sound funny. But I believe it to be a dangerous belief. Contrary to science, you cannot abrogate the laws of physics!' His arms were doing their best to abrogate every law known to science. 'No matter how much faith you have, if there is a brick up there and it's coming straight down on my head you cannot by faith affect the trajectory of the thing.' Both hands shot above his head to catch the falling brick.

I couldn't help myself. I said, 'The Bible says it rains on the just and the unjust.'

'Well,' said Magnus, hurling the brick back into space, 'the Bible's got a lot of sense in it, but these superstitions which are encrusting us roundabout' – the fingers of both hands clawed at the crust – 'are distinctly menacing. Science is so different. Take chemistry. You know perfectly well that if you mix substance A with substance B you will get nylon.' The nylon is stretched to its limits. 'It's never existed before, but you will always get it, if you do it right.

'If you switch on the switch and the Central Electricity Board has done its business right, you get electricity. And,' the left hand pointed back into history, 'it knew its business because of Michael Faraday, who said if you have a moving wire through a magnetic force you will get electricity – and you will *always* get electricity. But you can go to some superstitious society which thinks electricity is magic.' One hand waved a wand, the other cast a spell. 'It isn't magic at all! It's using your wits! Take biology.' He looked around as if expecting to discover a small box marked, 'Biology'. 'Smallpox used to come as an absolute curse; people would go down on their knees!' He stopped and pointed at a spot on the carpet; we both stared at it in horror. 'Not at all! By using biology and collecting the evidence, smallpox has been exterminated from the face of the earth!' A wild eye caught mine as if expecting a challenge.

I countered with a question. 'These are actually the things that you believe in, aren't they?'

'I believe them because they always happen.' He turned and appealed to an imaginary jury. 'There is so *much* evidence, every time I switch it on – electricity does come. If you make yourself a dynamo,' his hands immediately began to construct one, 'and you move wires through the fields of force, you have electricity every time – not just occasionally!'

I thought it might be worth a shot, so I said, 'Is there any *mystery* in your life?'

'Oh dear.' Both hands covered his face. He appeared to be a man on the verge of total despair. 'Well, coming on to faith I would like, as it were, to be an honourable, kindly man.' The hands undulated, gentle waves, lapping on the shore. 'I would like that. As an act of faith, maybe I would do much better, be a better scientist. I am an absolute brute.' Clenched fists beat on an invisible door.

I said, 'How do you know what a kindly man is? What is a good man?'

'I am prepared to change chairs with you. I have a – *feeling*' – the arms hugged him, against his will – 'that I do know, and that's all I can say.' He broke free from the hug, but was immediately embraced again. 'And I have a *feeling* that I *do* know what is kindliness.' An arm pointed to a person somewhere in the distance. 'Of course, you get the parent who whacks the child,' a hand whacked the air, 'who says, "I am not going to kill you with kindness" – which is quite a different thing. It does not mean that. Because I believe in science.' He pointed to the carpet once again, and we stared at it, 'I do *not* believe what these credulous people, writing the back page of the *Sun*, believe. It doesn't mean that science fills the *whole* of my consciousness or governs *all* my actions.'

'Would you say that you believed in God?'

'It depends what you mean by God.'

(How did I know he was going to say that?)

'Here.' An arm indicated where. 'We have this marvellous system. If I had time, I would tell you that I was sitting next to the man who by science,' he draws science on the wall, 'deduced the date of the origin of the universe.' The arms cannot resist 'the universe'. 'I believe in a God who has created this extraordinary and wonderful system.' Two hands karate chop an imaginary log. 'Yes! And presumably it is something I believe in by faith, and it makes me want to behave well.' Another karate chop. 'Yes! To that extent I do. But I don't believe in somebody with a long beard who's going to change the rules of science. If it's a miracle,' the hands push a massive boulder over a cliff, 'I don't believe it! A miracle, by its very definition, is different from the laws of nature.'

'So you believe in a creator.'

'Yes, I do, in a rather misty way.' His body sways and he seems to get quite close to levitation. 'Because this total cosmos, the universe, the cosmos is so strange.' He shifted a gear and the hands went into hyper drive. Everything was drawn, circled, scythed, underlined and described in great circles and rectangles of blurred movement. You see, light travels at certain speeds, as you are well aware. As we are whizzing round and round the sun, as you go towards light, you would think you would go fast as you went towards it and slow as you went away from it, wouldn't you? But scientists discovered that this is a cock-eyed world. Whether you are going towards it, or away from it, the speed of light is *exactly* the same. It's like a sock pulled out of shape.' He pulled an imaginary sock further than any sock has ever been pulled, '*that's* what the universe is. Now I find it marvellous and I feel a great reverence when these sorts of things are brought to our attention, discovered,' the arms lifted high above his head, 'by scientists.'

I look up and, for the first time, I am aware that the angels – archangels, guardian angels, cherubim and seraphim – are all wearing white coats, looking into microscopes and singing Pythagoras' theorem in four-part harmony.

Agnostic Fish

We left the M1 at junction 6A and headed west along the M25. We didn't have much further to go. At the Rickmansworth exit we would leave the motorway and head for Joan and Desmond Martin's riverside cottage. We had first met Joan at the Hayes Conference Centre, at a Methodist School of Fellowship summer holiday conference, when I was a theological student in the sixties. Gosh! The sixties, flower power, the Beatles, and psychedelic shirts.

The 'A41 – Exit 20 in one mile' sign warned those who wanted to go to Tring and Aylesbury that this might be a good time to pull over into the slow lane and start slowing down. Most people do, some leave it to the half-mile sign, and there are others who feel that the only method of leaving a motorway is to wait until the last possible moment, cut across two lanes of traffic, bump over the white chevrons separating motorway from slip road and then stand on their brakes when they reach the roundabout at the top of the exit road.

June, who was driving, said, 'Do you think Magnus Pyke is an agnostic?'

I said, 'I think it all depends on how you define the word "agnostic". Generally speaking, most people think of an agnostic as someone who is uncommitted or uncertain about the existence of God, but there is another use of the word "agnostic" as meaning those who think that nothing is known, or can be known, about the existence or nature of God, that is they think God is "unknowable". I think Magnus might come into that category. He is not sitting on the fence and saying, "I don't know if God exists or not." I think he is prepared to allow for the existence of intelligent purpose within the creative process, but not a "person" or a being with a personality that can be known and related to. I think there is a lot to be said in defence of the *genuine* agnostic. The genuine agnostic does not sit *comfortably* on the fence. Sitting comfortably on the fence is usually an excuse for avoiding serious thought of any kind. But a genuine agnostic is someone who, after a great deal of thought and discussion, finds they are not sitting, but stuck, uncomfortably – on the fence.'

I reached for our massive, large-scale *A to Z of London*. 'Do you think Rickmansworth will be in this *A to Z*?'

June said, 'Yes, I think it is. Not that we need it. I know the way.' She was absolutely right, we both knew the way. Reaching for the big *A to Z* the moment you drive on the London side of the M25 has become automatic. I shoved the book back in its place.

'Actually,' she said, 'anybody who continues to ask serious questions about the meaning of life is, inevitably – to some extent – agnostic, I suppose. In fact, it's not the people who don't know all the answers who worry me so much as the people who think they do know all the answers.'

'Yes,' I said, 'and jumping off the fence does not mean that you automatically fall into the supportive arms of faith. It can be, for some people, a nerve-wracking step into the dark, the beginning of a perilous exploration of a vast, uncharted continent. What information there is, is confused by tales told by slightly unhinged travellers; and there are witch doctors, and centuries of ancient myth. It's like searching for the source of a great river with thousands of tributaries – and up every tributary there are wild-eyed explorers shouting, "It's here! It's here!" And sometimes you are pitched out of your canoe into the swirling waters of doubt and cynicism.'

June said, 'What would you say, then, was the difference between the searching agnostic and the searching believer?'

'Well,' I said, 'if we can stay up the river with the tributaries, I would say that the agnostic in his canoe says, "I have not yet seen any light to indicate the direction in which I should travel." Whereas the believer says, "It is a bit dark where I am, too, but I believe I can see something, up ahead!"'

'Yes, so can I,' June said. 'It's Exit 18, Rickmansworth.' The 300-yards sign came into view and June flicked down the indicator. 'Staying in the water, or going under it, rather, I think Anthony de Mello's "fish" story is on similar lines to your searching believers and agnostics in their canoes.'

'Which story is that?'

'The one about a little fish swimming in the sea, who is searching for the ocean. He swims a very long way asking all the time, "Where is the ocean?" Eventually he meets a wise old fish who says to him, "The ocean? Where is the ocean? You are in it. It's *under* you – and *over* you. It's the very life that passes through your gills."'

'The searching agnostic fish,' I said. 'I like that idea, and I like the idea of God not being something up ahead, or beyond you, but all around you, and in you.'

Soundings

We were on the Rickmansworth by-pass and June said, 'When you asked Magnus what was the basis of his faith in science, he said, more or less, that it lay in the fact that if you complete a mathematical equation, or follow a known formula in a chemistry laboratory, the result will always be the same. You can repeat it over and over and it will work every time, because science is about the observation of verifiable facts. OK, so far so good, but does that mean there are no such things as spiritual values? Do you say that if you cannot see, touch, measure or weigh things, they don't exist? Surely, having a spiritual understanding of life is what gives it quality, meaning, depth?'

The trouble with television conversations is that when the studio floor manager, standing out of sight of the guest's eye-line, but directly in yours, counts down the last thirty seconds and then draws his forefinger dramatically across his throat, the conversation comes to an end, no matter how interesting it is getting, or how long you could have gone on exploring the subject. In one way, the conversation with Magnus Pyke stopped just when it was getting particularly interesting, to me at any rate.

'To be fair to Magnus,' I said, 'he did imply that there was more to being a human being than simply measuring and observing material phenomena, when he said he had a "feeling" about what was right and wrong; and again, when he said that looking at the universe gave him a "misty" sense of intelligence behind it all. I think at that point he was on the verge of grappling with spiritual values.'

June said, 'Would you say that music and art embrace spirituality better than words can? After all, subtle colours and intricate harmonies can say things that words couldn't hope to capture. Doesn't the artist explore depth and meaning in ways that scientific equations can't?'

'I wouldn't write off words and language altogether. I think some people, poets for instance, can use words as musicians and artists use colours and chords. I think poetry probably works best when it opens up our imaginations and take us on a trip beyond the literal meaning of the words used.'

'It's down this lane on the left, isn't it?' She signalled and began to slow. A BMW from nowhere cut across our bows.

'Yes, it is, I think. Yes, there's the finger sign on the other side of the road.'

She turned into the lane. 'On the other hand,' she said, 'St Paul believed that words couldn't touch every depth. In fact, isn't that why we need spirituality? To interpret our "inexpressible" prayers in, what was it he said, "groans too deep for words"?'

I laughed. 'Yes, even if that passage is in itself an example of the kind of poetry I was talking about. I suppose if, at this point, our scientist friends were to say, "Ah, you are now wandering off, out of the real world of facts into the fantasy world of imagination," we would have to reply, "But men and women have the ability to see visions, to dream dreams." All human beings have imaginations. It is a quintessential quality of being human, isn't it? Our imaginations open up doors to understanding the meaning of things, so it would be irresponsible and illogical to repudiate creative flights of imagination because they were not measurable, quantifiable or repeatable. To the religious, "prayer" is an instrument of spiritual adventure, through which the pilgrim might soar free or, in contemplation, sound depths that enrich the soul. But who can provide a formula to guarantee a repeat of the same spiritual experience? I can't, but that doesn't mean that spiritual experiences don't happen.'

June said, 'Good. There's a space on the drive at this end of the cottage.' She pulled into the drive. You have to stop pretty accurately or you end up in the river.

June put the gear lever into 'P' for 'Parking', and I said, 'I suppose I am using language that Magnus would describe as poetic licence running wild, but I have to ask . . .' My window slid down of its own accord, or more likely at the bidding of June's right hand on the window controls. Being in full flight, I continued without a pause. 'Who,' I said, 'could formulate an equation that could measure, weigh or evaluate the breath of the Spirit, on which, and through which, in every human tongue, the traffic of the world's prayers are carried? I can't, I doubt if anyone could, nevertheless, I still believe that the breath of God is the essence of life itself, of existence.' I became aware of a face smiling at me through the now completely open window.

'Very poetic,' said Joan. 'Did you have a good journey?'

Infinite God, you are 'a sea without a shore, a sun without a sphere'
yet through groans too deep for words, your Holy Spirit
admits us into the mystery of your being,
whose essence is love and healing and peace.
For all your mercies, Lord, we give you thanks. Amen.

3   God's Truth

It Ain't Necessarily So!

We were now passing Oxted, to the south of us, a place I could never pass without mentally bowing my head in acknowledgment of the friendship I had enjoyed with Stuart Jackman, who had at one time been the URC minister at Oxted. Stuart Jackman had also written perhaps the most controversial Passion-play of the twentieth century, *The Davidson Affair*. I will also always remember, with affection, our partnership together at the BBC, when we had worked on a series called 'Conversations with my Conscience'. I had not realised at the time that my life in broadcasting, both on radio and on television, was to be filled with conversations about people's consciences or, in some cases, an apparent *lack* of conscience.

I spoke to one man whose conscience was at ease with the idea of running a mail order agency for Malaysian brides, and another chap who ran a kind of security firm who didn't balk at the idea of kidnapping someone. In fact, they were involved with kidnapping Ronnie Biggs, the great train robber, and when I said, 'Do you have your own morality about which jobs you take and which jobs you don't?' he had said, 'Yes. I will take jobs which pay money.'

I think he saw it all as an exciting adventure, fun. When I was a child I saw a Laurel and Hardy film which was called *Shanghaied* in which a sea captain, anxious to obtain a crew, arranged to have men 'shanghaied' as they came out of a sailors' tavern. It was meant to be funny, but as a child I was horrified about the kidnapped men, their wives, their children and instead of laughing it made me feel quite upset. Perhaps I was an over-sensitive child who didn't see kidnapping as entertaining or amusing. I still don't.

Once, on television, I spoke to Jill Morrell, John McCarthy's girlfriend at the time of his kidnap in Beirut. When I spoke to her, John McCarthy was in his fourth year in captivity. Jill had initiated a campaign called 'Friends of John McCarthy'. She was trying to keep his case in the public eye, trying to keep his situation before the Government. The Government had of course had a policy of, 'We don't do business with terrorists' and Jill didn't disagree with that, but she felt that the Government should be doing something, and it appeared to her that they were doing absolutely nothing whatsoever. When she started the campaign, it was a complete act of faith. At that time she did not know if John was still alive; she did not know what the kidnappers wanted; she did not know if there was a price on his head, or not. In fact, the first positive evidence that he was still alive did not come until the French hostages were released and they spoke of their knowledge of McCarthy.

Jill Morrell's campaign for John McCarthy also made people aware of Brian Keenan, the Irish hostage. It reminded the world of Terry Waite who, although he had originally been rather more well known than John McCarthy, had simply dropped out of public awareness, having been missing for two years. Jill never spoke about it publicly, but one of the pressures that must have been part of her life at that time was the fact that she was a young girl who had to keep the faith with someone who hadn't been seen for four years. She had no idea whether he was going to be released that year, next year or perhaps never. She knew she had to keep faith with him even though the years and her own youthfulness might possibly slip away before she saw him again. At the same time, she was aware that even if he was released their relationship might have changed. Even if he came back safe and sound, she knew that they would not be, in fact even now they were no longer, the same people. It is difficult to assess the courage this awful situation demanded of her, but it must have been considerable.

Back in the days of the Old Testament, one of the ways in which conquering regimes maintained power and completely demoralised a country they had conquered, and also removed all chance of there being a resistance movement rising up against them, was to take all the able-bodied men out of the country, to lose them, more or less, in one of their territories, putting them to work in some other part of the world so that there was no way they could start up a patriotic movement in their own country. Imagine the awful distress such action must have caused to those taken into captivity, and those left behind. As years went by, the invaders would have colonised the land they had captured and the captives who had been taken away would have been absorbed, slowly, into the society and the culture into which they had been taken.

However, when the people of Israel were taken captive and hauled off to Babylon, a faithful core of them maintained their identity by keeping strictly to the laws of their faith. They refused to marry; they refused to worship false gods; they remained faithful to Israel and dreamed of the day when they would go back to Jerusalem, back to their own country. They kept close to their hearts and minds the great days of David. The high point of their history had been the rule of King David, so they dreamed and prayed and their prophets prophesied the coming of another king like David, a messiah who would throw out the invaders and restore the chosen people to their promised land.

I signalled and pulled out into the middle lane in order to pass an Eddie Stobart truck being driven sedately as ever, by one of their green-shirted and dark-tied drivers. When I had passed the Stobart truck, June said to me, 'What about the gender of God, and the fact that God is always referred to as "he"?'

We were one mile from Exit 9, the turn-off for Leatherhead. Leatherhead was absolutely laden with memories for both of us; we had met and married in Leatherhead. Our first professional jobs in the theatre had been with Leatherhead Repertory Theatre. It was in that town that we had explored drama from Euripides to Whitehall farce, from pantomime to Arthur Miller. John Wesley had also preached his last sermon in Leatherhead. I think we saw the sign simultaneously. There was no need to say anything. We just looked at each other and smiled.

'I think,' I said, 'calling God "he" is an indication of how limited our understanding of God is. It tells us more about human nature than it does about God. Christianity emerged out of Judaism and the God of Israel was an incredibly sophisticated concept. Look at the book of Genesis and imagine the period of history when that concept of God was put together. It was in the days when there were primitive tribespeople who lived in fear of a whole range of deities, gods of the sun, moon, stars, water and fire, gods of the harvest, and their own private, man-made tribal idols; whereas the sons and daughters of Abraham had a sophisticated concept of a God who was a spirit, who could not be seen, who was without form and whose very name was unutterable. The poetry at the beginning of the book of Genesis captures the concept beautifully, "In the beginning God created the heavens and the earth. Earth was without form and void and darkness was upon the face of the deep and the spirit of God was moving over the face of the waters." The story of the creation in the book of Genesis is both poetic and inspired, but it isn't always wise to take poetry literally. People often ask, "Is the Bible true?" In one sense it is not a proper question. The Bible is a collection of the writings of a particular culture through a period of two or three thousand years and there are saga poems and children's stories, epic adventure tales, hymns and songs. There are so many kinds of literature contained within the books of the Bible, and it is a library of books. You would not say of the literature of England from Chaucer to the present day, 'Is it true?' It would not be an appropriate question. But if you asked, "Does it contain the truth? Is it inspired? Does it embrace goodness, truth, love, integrity?" The answer is an emphatic, "Yes, it does."

'For me, the only way in which one can begin to understand the Bible is to look at the truth contained within the stories, but not to look at the stories in their detail and ask if the details are exactly right. It's the heart of the story, the content that has to be true; there has to be a revelation about the nature of life, the human race and God.

'Supposing I told you the tale of the shepherd boy who decided to spice up his day by shouting, "Wolf!" and had all the villagers rushing out with their pitchforks in order to chase off the wolf, only to find that the boy was playing a joke on them. When a second call came there must have been doubts in the minds of the villagers, but nevertheless they rushed out to see if a wolf was, in fact, attacking the sheep. On the third occasion, not surprisingly, the villagers refused to believe the boy, sadly for him, because this time there was a wolf, who came and devoured the sheep. The truth of that story is that if you tell lies ultimately you will suffer the consequences. If I changed all the details of the story and said that actually it wasn't a boy, it was a girl and she wasn't looking after sheep, she was looking after goats, none of these details would alter the content of the story. I could change the details in many different ways and it wouldn't matter as long as I didn't alter the heart of the story. In the story of the creation, in Genesis, the truth is contained in the very first words, "In the beginning, God created the heavens and the earth.' I believe the Bible to be the inspired word of God, inspired poetry, inspired imagery, inspired storytelling, but poetry and storytelling need, above all, a freedom of expression in order to capture and present the essence of the truth.

'Jesus taught in parables; he used allegories, imagined stories. Was there a man set upon by robbers on the road to Jericho? Or was Jesus simply telling a story in order to make clear a truth he was trying to teach? Was there a prodigal son for whom the father waited? Or was Jesus trying to teach about the nature of God? If the writers of the Old Testament, in their attempts to express the might and the power of Almighty God, began to use masculine words – words associated with warriors and fierce, powerful, sword-wielding, muscle-bound men – what it reveals as much as anything else was the failure of their poetry to embrace insight into the wholeness of God. They found it difficult to conceive of a God who was vulnerable, or a God who had attributes related to femininity, and qualities that are associated with gentleness, nurturing and motherhood. To this day people conceive of power in terms of might. There are very few people who conceive of power in terms of love. Yet a God without feminine qualities is necessarily a deficient concept. Making God "male" seems to me to be a betrayal of that wonderful vision with which the book of Genesis starts, the vision of God as a spirit, moving on the face of the deep – a concept of God which simply cannot be contained by a name, image, or gender.

'One could argue that the whole of the Bible is a failure to put spiritual experience, spiritual insight into workaday, earthy, comprehensible language. My mother, who was a very good storyteller, would not hesitate to embellish a true story if she thought it would bring out more of the essence of that story. There is a theory that if you want to understand history, the best books to read are books of fiction. The whole of history is coloured by political influence. Historians know which side their bread is buttered on and if you were the court historian for a particular king, you would write your history so that the king approved of it. The Bible is no different. Look closely and you find there are stories about kings who were not particularly good kings but they were very good sons of Israel. As a result they get a good write-up. But if there is a king, who may have been an excellent king, but was not someone who lived faithfully by the law of God, then he might merit no more than a paragraph or two.

'If your understanding of the Battle of Hastings is of the noble, last stand of Harold, you ought to go over to Bayeux and look at the tapestry there and see the stories told in the Bayeux museum, and you will find that the French view of that event is quite different from the English one.

'When I worked for Granada Television, I once met Mark Lane. Mark Lane was the defence lawyer who represented Lee Harvey Oswald. Now, the world might have been informed that Lee Harvey Oswald was the assassin of President Kennedy, but an hour with Mark Lane made me perfectly convinced that whoever killed President Kennedy, it was not Lee Harvey Oswald. He presented such convincing evidence. There was a very famous picture that was flashed around the world of Oswald the gunman with a rifle in his hand. Mark Lane pointed out that there were inconsistencies in the photograph. The shadow from the rifle was a long shadow, which suggested that when that photograph was taken the sun was low in the sky. The shadow under Oswald's nose is straight down, directly underneath his nose, which suggests that when the photograph was taken the sun was almost directly over head. In other words, it was a composite photograph, it was put together by someone. I was left absolutely convinced that the history books had been manipulated.

'Years ago, Malcolm Muggeridge was asked to make a recording to go into a time capsule for a hundred years. He said, "Dear historian of the twenty-first century, how excited you must be as you open up the time capsule. Here you must feel is the key to the twentieth century. I am afraid I have to disappoint you. We have no idea what is going on. And if *we* do not know what is going on, how on earth can you hope to understand what actually happened in this, our century?"

'On the other hand, the writers of stories, of sagas, of fictions are not vetted, they are not censored by politicians, editors and adapters. The good novelist will capture the essence of the history of the time and the place of a particular era in a way that historians may not be allowed to. It is said that Charles Dickens captured the essence of his period. Some people said that he exaggerated, he painted pictures which were slightly larger than life, that some of his characters were too eccentric, too oddly behaved. Yet the curious thing is that recently the remains of two Victorian sailors were found in the ice of the North-west Passage, in the frozen wastes of the Arctic circle. It presented a very exciting opportunity to conduct a post mortem on two Victorian bodies with all the advantages and advances of modern forensic science. It was discovered that they had died of hypothermia, but both of them had been suffering from quite severe lead poisoning. The likelihood is that most people in Dickens's day were suffering to a greater or lesser extent from lead poisoning. One of the side effects of lead poisoning is eccentric behaviour. Dickens did not have to invent eccentric characters. They existed all around him. All he had to do was to describe the people he saw, met and talked with each and every day of his life. All writers, artists and musicians have struggled with the same problem for centuries. "How can I capture the essence in my story, in my picture, in my song?" Writers in the Bible were faced with exactly the same problem.'

June was looking pensive and then she said, 'If lead poisoning produces eccentric behaviour, do you think the number of hours we've spent on the road, drinking in lead poison, from the exhausts of millions of motor-cars, might just possibly lead us to be considered slightly eccentric?'

'An interesting theory,' I said. 'Except that you and I are both so eminently sane.'

She considered this and said, 'Staines and Heathrow. Would you like an apple?'

Casting Stones

The signs for 'the North' had appeared and there was a lifting of the spirits at the thought that we would soon be leaving the M25.

'All things considered,' I said, 'it hasn't been a bad M25 run today.'

'No, it hasn't,' said June. 'Shall we see what's on the news?'

'Good idea. If you put it on now it might give some traffic news.'

What we got, in fact, was a weather forecast from Michael Fish, in which we learned that some places would be dry and some wet, and the outlook promised more of the same. It reminded me of a morning when I was a continuity announcer at BBC Radio Bristol, alone in the building in the early hours, waiting for the 'rip-and-read' news service machine to spew out a weather forecast. In a few minutes I would have to run down a flight of stairs, throw myself at a self-op studio, take a deep breath and read the news I was, even at that moment, sub-editing, as I waited for the weather. The seconds ticked by. There were fourteen stairs to descend, three spring-loaded doors to heave open and pass through, and several knobs and dials to turn before saying, after the Greenwich time signal, 'Good morning, it's six o'clock and here is the news from BBC Radio Bristol.'

The rip-and-read machine appeared to have switched itself off permanently. There was nothing for it. I scrabbled in the waste bin, found last night's forecast, looked out of the window and did as intelligent an update as I could and then started to run for the stairs. As the newsroom door hissed behind me I heard the rip-and-read burst into life. It was too late now, I was committed. As it turned out, my forecast of 'wet in places, dry in others' and my suggestion that the 'outlook' would probably be 'more of the same', turned out to be fairly accurate, strangely.

The news on the car radio was informing us that a Catholic bishop had admitted being the father of a love-child some twenty-five years earlier. When I was a small boy there was a man who used to walk up and down the Pier Head, in Liverpool, wearing a sandwich board, which said on one side, 'Be sure your sins will find you out'. This used to worry me. 'Does this mean my mother will find out that I've licked the jam knife?' (Knife-licking was forbidden – *absolutely*.) These things weigh heavily on your mind when you're six years old. Of course, nowadays you could rewrite that text as, 'If you ever go into public life be sure the newspapers will find out your sins'. Whether you are a bishop who made a mistake a quarter of a century ago, or whether you are acknowledged as one of the legendary heroes or saints of the age, like Nelson Mandela or Archbishop Tutu, if you have done something as human as falling in love, having rows or making errors of judgment, you may be sure the media will make the most of it. There is nothing more attractive to a news editor than the fallen idol.

Gerald Priestland, who collected headlines, and had a display of them pinned to his office notice-board, suggested that the ideal headline for the sensationalist tabloid editor would contain a combination of words about violence – preferably murder, sex, money and the aristocracy – which might produce headlines that read something like, 'Sex-change Nun Killed – Millionaire Duke Arrested'. I can't remember the exact wording, but at the time of our conversation Gerry had pointed to a headline in his private collection of 'headline shockers', that was not a million miles away from the case of the 'nun and the duke' story.

I saw a programme on TV about Dr Albert Schweitzer,

the man who built and ran a hospital in an equatorial African jungle for more than forty years. The programme voiced criticisms of Albert Schweitzer, which implied that he was a bit of a colonialist in his attitude and his approach to Africans would certainly fall short of modern, political correctness. For heaven's sake! The man was born in 1875! He could have made a fortune in any career he chose. He was a world-famous organist. He wrote a book still considered a classic on Bach. He was a university professor, had a degree in theology and was a qualified surgeon, but he chose to spend his life nursing the sick in equatorial Africa. As evidence of his flawed character there was a woman in the television programme who said, 'In the end he became quite vain you know. When the press photographers came, sometimes he would even put on a jacket.' Good heavens! Did the man have no shame?

When Jesus Christ was asked to judge someone's fall from grace he said, 'Let him who has no sin cast the first stone.' I suppose I must be grateful that I am not a professional stone-thrower, though come to think of it I've just heaved a rather large brick at news editors, but there we are, nobody's perfect.

The Methodist church in the Square in Dunstable is huge. There is no other adequate word for it. Words like 'ample', 'large', 'spacious', would all fall short, 'huge' is the only word. We had asked for a platform. A platform had been constructed to sit on top of the first six or seven rows of pews and there was still room for a considerable audience to assemble, not only downstairs but also in the equally cavernous gallery above. If ever the UK were to become a republic and Bedfordshire an independent state, the senators would do well to consider the Methodist church in Dunstable for their senate house.

Our lighting tripods and tee-bars were assembled in the gallery. Sound-system speakers were strapped to balcony rails and miles of cable neatly stowed and taped. It is always a source of wonder to me that before an audience begins to arrive cables seem to have disappeared and lighting and sound systems have somehow been absorbed into the fabric of the building. So that even if your eye does focus on them they give the appearance of always having been there. It takes two or three hours to rig up the equipment and about an hour and a half to derig. In the peculiar quiet of a large and echoing building in the middle of the afternoon gazing at row after row of seating, certain thoughts cross your mind. Will a goodly number fill those seats? Will the technical equipment work? Will the magic happen yet again? In the hour before curtain up, life begins to enter the building, footsteps on wooden floors, people greeting each other, teacups rattling as refreshments are prepared in adjoining rooms, where urns hiss and bubble.

In the last minutes the overture is playing and the air is filled with the excitement of a talking, laughing, expectant audience. The actor's adrenaline begins to stir and in the vestry dressing-room the deep-breathing exercises begin.

It was a wonderful night. The empty rows were filled downstairs and up in the gallery, I could see it and feel it. The house lights are extinguished, the stage lighting slowly fades, the hubbub of the audience is stilled and before a word is spoken, the mysterious excitement, the enchantment, the spell of theatre has gently cloaked all of us.

The Kingdom of God Is Like . . .

In the morning we were in no particular hurry to leave Dunstable; we wanted to arrive at the M25 well after the rush hours had passed. We opted for the clockwise route eastward towards the wonderful Dartford Bridge. I was driving and June was leafing through the morning paper.

'I keep seeing articles,' she said, 'that say British people work longer hours than anyone else in Western society. It's not that they want to work long hours; it's fear. Fear that they will lose their jobs, be passed over, made redundant. Apparently some organisations think they can achieve most by keeping people in fear of losing their jobs, but there is evidence that some of the most profitable companies are those with a genuine concern with the welfare of their employees. When companies honestly try to assist people to achieve their own personal goals, to meet family needs and encourage them in their hopes and ambitions, you actually get a happier and more efficient work force and consequently bigger profits.

'Today there is a report on a survey done by the Institute of Management which says that in British business and industry at every level, from management to shop floor, people are stressed out or demoralised. Restructuring, or cost-cutting by another name, has resulted in fewer people doing more and more work under even greater pressure, which in turn produces more people suffering from anxiety and depression, none of which is actually very good for business. All this suggests that there is something not quite right in the way that things are being run.'

'That reminds me of Lance, the New Zealander. Do you remember him?' I said. 'He worked for a company in London which kept halving the workforce and expecting the remaining half to do the same amount of work. Which is not all that far removed from Christopher Fry's, *The First Born*. In that play, the people of Israel, enslaved by the Pharaohs of Egypt, had their workload doubled. They were ordered not only to make the bricks for the Pharaoh's building but, in addition, to cut the straw to make the bricks, and at the same time they were expected to achieve the same quota of bricks as before. Not much seems to have changed in the last five thousand years, has it? We are, it seems, as far away as ever from establishing the kingdom of God on earth.'

June said, 'What about those Jesuit ruins we visited in the Missione area, in South America? That must have come pretty close.'

'Oh, yes,' I said. 'You're absolutely right. That was an attempt to establish the kingdom of God on earth, and you could also say that for a hundred and fifty years it worked.'

The Jesuits had established a community which pooled its resources, skills, talents and crafts and shared out the results of all labour according to people's needs. People put in according to their ability and took out according to their needs. Some people were born, lived and died in that community. The community would have continued had it not been for the Spanish colonialists deciding that the best thing to do was to get rid of the Jesuits and break up their communities because they were standing in the way of their land-grabbing operations.'

June said, 'Do you remember the rainstorm?'

'Do I remember the rainstorm? Who could forget?' We were in a car then. To be in a rainstorm in a tropical rainforest is an event that has to be seen and experienced to be believed: sheets of rain so dense that we had to stop the car; a curtain of water in front of us and another being driven across the surface of the road; and the noise, as the rain hit the car, absolutely deafening.

June said, 'Look, our first Eddie Stobart of the day.' As we passed the Eddie Stobart truck, June said, 'Do you think the kingdom of God on earth is possible, or is it just wishful thinking?'

'Well,' I said, 'the fact that it worked for a few hundred years in South America indicates that it could work, but throughout history people seem to have pursued power – physical, political or financial power – and all that that has produced is a world in which there is a huge divide between rich and poor; a world in which at any one time there are usually eight or nine or more wars of one kind or another being fought in different parts of the globe.

'I suppose it's the ultimate lack of faith, really. Lack of faith that a world ruled by love could actually work. When Jesus was teaching about the kingdom of God, all the values of his kingdom seemed to be the opposite of all the values of the kingdoms of our world.

'The kingdom of God, in fact, turns the wisdom of our world on its head. For instance, in the kingdom of God, money and possessions are for giving away and for sharing, rather than keeping. Success is measured in terms of serving rather than ruling, wealth is distributed not according to our ability to earn but according to need and the demands of love and mercy. According to the example in a parable that Jesus once told, in the kingdom of God, workers who were only able to do a little were to be paid as much as those who were to be paid a lot. And if we say, "But that's not fair, that's not just," it's worth remembering that in the kingdom of God we do not receive what is just, or what we deserve, but we receive generosity and mercy, because that is what the kingdom of God is about.

'Yet it seems that the normal human response to any proposition, for any kind of kingdom, any way of life, is, "What's in it for me?" Every year when we hear the Budget, the most important bits are the bits that affect me, my life. The unspoken question is always there, "What's in it for me? What am I personally going to get out of it?"

'Ivan Turgenev once wrote a passage in a novel in which two characters discuss the idea of there being something higher than happiness, and one suggests that it is love but not love the pleasure, but love the sacrifice. But the other says he doesn't want to make sacrifices, he wants love for himself. "I want to be number one." And the first character says, "Number one, really? I feel that one's whole destiny in life is to be number two."

'Which is of course an echo of Jesus saying that if you live for self you'll die, but if you die to yourself you live. Ultimately you can only find happiness when you lose yourself in someone or something else. Or when we stop asking, "What's in it for me?" and start asking, "What's in it for him, or her, or them?"

'I did a piece once, on the *Terry Wogan Show*, about the kingdom of God. It was in response to an article that Miles Kingston had written in the *Independent*, in which he had suggested that in the General Election, Jesus would have been the ideal anti-sleaze candidate. He wasn't being blasphemous. He was simply drawing the readers' attention to the difference in style and content between what our politicians preach and what Jesus preached. Which made me wonder what kind of manifesto Jesus might have produced if he had been standing for an election. I think he might have said, "I don't simply want your vote, but your commitment. If you support my party, I will actually expect you to feed the hungry and visit the sick because my party stands for *doing* the will of my Heavenly Father, not *talking* about it. Your votes are not about giving me power; they are about you empowering the powerless, the widow, the fatherless, the poor, the homeless."'

The Jesus Party Manifesto

The keynote of my manifesto is simply this, '*Love One Another*'.

But it is a radical kind of love, '*Love in Action*' you could say. When I say that I want you to 'love your neighbour', I don't mean blow him kisses; I mean, clothe him, and give him shelter. Now as we are on this tack, let's have a look at some of my other policies.

Defence Policy: Or as I prefer to call it, the 'turn the other cheek' policy. Basically my party believes that all enemies are to be loved.

Wages and Employment: From my experience in vineyards, I am determined that everybody should receive the same wage, whatever their input.

Law and Order: We believe that you should 'judge not' and not be judged. And forgiveness should be available to all, immediately on request.

Housing: In my Father's house there are many mansions, built on rock, of course.

Social Security: Entitlements to benefits – the requirements are, basically,

1. Knocking on a door, which will be opened.
2. Asking, which will automatically entitle you to receive.

Benefits will include

1. For the heavy-laden, rest.
2. For the troubled and distressed, peace beyond all understanding.

To sum up, we believe that 'love in action' is the answer to all the world's problems. It is not a soft option. This kind of love is costly and demanding. This love, we believe, is the answer to hunger, it is the answer to poverty, it is the answer to war. In fact, we think it is the kind of love that actually makes the world go round.

So, why not *join the Jesus Party* and vote for Jesus. *You know it makes sense.*

I think G.K. Chesterton knew the size of it, when he was talking about Christianity as a way of life, and said, 'Christianity has not been tried and found wanting. It has been found difficult and not tried.' Never a truer word.

4   To Be a Pilgrim

True Valour

It might sound self-evident, but one of the most enjoyable and enriching aspects of travelling to myriad places and events – to cities, towns and hamlets, getting involved in church festivals and anniversaries, theatre enterprises, village hall celebrations, radio and television series – is that, inevitably, we meet a great many people with fascinating stories to tell.

For a number of years I was involved in a network television series that was recorded in the Yorkshire Television studios in Leeds. It involved travelling from Kent to Leeds each week. Eventually, we thought it would make more sense to live a little nearer to the Yorkshire Television studios. So we moved to a romantic spot in North Wales. No sooner had we done that than the series came to an end, and in addition I fell ill, quite seriously it seemed at the time. In retrospect, if you have, somehow or other, managed to survive the outrageous slings and arrows, you can be philosophical and view all the pitfalls and ironies as character-building experiences, giving colour and depth to life's rich and intricate tapestry. But at the time, when the earth is actually opening up beneath you, anyone uttering platitudes along these lines would receive very short shrift indeed.

If, however, we had begun to think that our days were littered with sudden and dramatic ups and downs, compared with some of the people I talked to in the television series, our gypsy wanderings about the English countryside appear idyllic, calm and relatively uneventful.

Someone who survived rather more than his fair share of tricky situations and still came up smiling was a man named John Campbell. John had served in Popski's Private Army during the war. After the war he became a fisherman only to see his chief asset, his schooner, sink beneath the waves one stormy night. He then joined the colonial service just in time for the Mau Mau uprising.

When I first met him, he was up to his neck in the Italian earthquake in Naples. The awesome figure of Her Britannic Majesty's Consul General for Naples and Sicily could be seen, with his sleeves rolled up, laying shuttering to make concrete bases for the temporary homes of earthquake victims.

In his sixties, he and his wife Shirley embarked on adventure which involved him in yet another situation in which, from time to time, he was required to roll up his sleeves and get down to work – mending holes in the road or in factory floors with his Rapid Repair Company.

We had spent a number of evenings, in places as far apart as Naples in Southern Italy and Leominster in Herefordshire, wrestling with questions about the unpredictability of life and the unreliability of events in general. It wasn't entirely surprising that we ended up discussing it all on television.

One of the admirable things about John Campbell is his irrepressible optimism and almost inexhaustible ability to find things to be grateful for. In that television programme I suggested to him that there couldn't have been much to feel grateful for, working behind the lines in Italy during the Second World War, to which he had replied, 'On the contrary, there was a tremendous amount. For the first time in the whole war, instead of just being frightened, it was also exciting. The second thing was that we were a very small unit and one experienced a close companionship and fellowship with people; and the third, and perhaps the most important thing, was that it brought me in to close contact with the Italian people and engendered a love for them that has never died.'

'Even though, at that time,' I said, 'they were your enemies?'

'No,' he said. 'By the time I got there they weren't enemies. They had already become "co-belligerents". The ones I met were more likely to be partisans and people who were fighting, or hated Mussolini.'

'After that experience,' I said, 'after the trauma of the war, you left the forces to launch yourself, if you'll pardon the expression, into business as a fisherman. Now, that was a pretty disastrous adventure. It ended, I seem to remember, quite literally on the rocks with you and your business partner being rescued on one of those chair-lift things. You had invested everything into that schooner; when she sank you lost every penny you had. That surely must have been a disaster that you were happy to put behind you and forget?'

He didn't hesitate. 'No. Certainly not. That adventure was perhaps one of the greatest experiences of the lot. Every day we felt we had achieved something. We worked alongside Irish fishermen, who you might think would never accept us, but we became close friends. It also brought us into close harmony with the elements, which is a very quick way of learning to be thankful that you're alive.'

'Is it fair,' I asked, 'to say that you are an exceptionally resilient man? You seem to be able to bounce up after disasters from which other people would find it impossible to bounce back.'

'I suppose to a certain extent that's true,' he said, 'but one is looking in a few minutes at a lifetime. In a lifetime you have many downs, many downs indeed. For example, sitting with Pat Blake – the night we lost the big boat, out there near Rathlin Island with a storm coming up and a mist over the sea, and we had fired all our security lights, the flares –

hoping that the lifeboat would come. We were jolly near the end then. But there hasn't always been something coming to the rescue at once, by any means.'

'Pat Blake was your comrade in Popski's Private Army, wasn't he?'

'Yes, he was. Then he came with me after the war, and even in my fourth career he has been a great tower of strength and help to me in many, many ways.'

'I suppose one of the benefits of shared adventures, even those which turn out to be disastrous, is that you create friendships which last a lifetime.'

'I think that is very true indeed.'

'Do you see yourself,' I asked, 'as a lucky, or an unlucky person?'

John Campbell smiled, a very broad smile. 'I would say that I was enormously lucky. I've got a wonderful wife and family, I've got everything that I really need and I've had a very exciting and eventful life. It hasn't seemed like that to other people though. For example, Jim Carney, who was an Irish boat-builder, once said to my mother, "If John was to buy Glasnevin Cemetery" (that's the biggest cemetery in Dublin), "sure nobody would die".'

'After you had lost your entire worldly fortune, when all your capital assets sank beneath the waves, you joined the colonial service in time for the Mau Mau uprising, which was a dreadful experience, certainly from what we read of it here. I would have thought that must have been a shattering experience.'

'The extraordinary thing is that out of all these dark events, things of exceptional value emerged. Many people who worked in the emergency in Kenya had never had direct contact with the Kikuyu people. At that time the Kikuyu had a reputation that meant they were generally despised as being cowards and horrible people, but it was not true. One learned that the vast majority were wonderful people. I came not only to admire them but I made many, many friends, to whom I could go back, tomorrow.'

'You ended up your diplomatic career in Italy, when we met during that awful earthquake. I remember visiting a village in the mountains, in winter; in fact you arranged it for me. The village was San Gregorio Magna, where some people were living in shacks and even cardboard boxes covered with plastic sheeting. I remember being appalled by that. What did that experience do for you?'

'Well, it was the first time I was really able to do something for the Italian people. Driving around in a car with a flag on it and meeting the prefects, the generals and admirals is fun, to a certain extent, but doesn't bring you into close contact with the people. This did. We took responsibility for two villages and looked after them right through the aftermath of the earthquake. We got to know them all very, very intimately and made very close friendships, and you could see that you were doing something for people. I think that did cement personal relationships and indeed national relationships as well.'

'John,' I said, 'you have gone from being driven around in a car with a flag on the front to, well, in your own words, "digging holes in the road". Do you feel that fate has let you down?'

'Indeed not. This is one of the most exciting experiences of my life. We've moved on a little from digging holes. What we are doing is bringing new techniques to things that have been done by traditional methods, with a very small firm. Therefore we have close-knit friendships, the same team spirit as in the consulate, in Popski's Private Army, or in a small boat in a storm. To me, all these things were, and are, just wonderful. I am, I suppose, an absolutely incurable optimist but, in the end, I think optimism is simply the ability to find enjoyment – even when things seem to be going wrong.'

Talk about 'dust yourself down and start all over again'. The thing that strikes me about John Campbell is that he

does not waste time trying to find someone to blame when
things go wrong, nor does he claim credit for all the good
things in his life. He is simply grateful for survival, grateful
for the chance to carry on, grateful for the gift of life itself.

Scallop, Staff and Scrip

During the run of the Yorkshire Television series, June and I
were booked into the Queen's Hotel in Leeds and most of
the guests who were to appear on the programme were also
booked into the same hotel. It was at the Queen's, the night
before the recording, that we had the most absorbing
conversations and, more often than not, hilarious evenings,
getting to know the people we would be working with the
following day.

Part of the excitement of each week lay in the fact that we
did not know, very far in advance, who we would dine with.
It could have been someone from almost any walk of life:
lawyers, politicians, trade unionists, bishops, musicians,
sportsmen and -women, peers of the realm or the occasional
film star.

One way or another, over the years, I have met and worked
with a great number of actors, singers and comedians, some
of whom have been star performers. One of the things that
successful performers of any ilk, from comedians to opera
singers, seem to have in common is a single-minded dedica-
tion to their careers. Keeping a high profile becomes an
obsession. Terry Thomas once confessed that in his early
days he spent a great deal of his earnings on hiring a public
relations company to promote his work. To survive in the
fleeting and fickle world of show business, one success must
be followed by another. The most important thing in life
becomes the next film, the next recording, the next concert,
the next tour.

I remember talking to Eric Morecambe, some time after

his heart attack. The experience had pulled him up short and made him review his priorities in a way he had not done before. He said that for years, most of his time had been absorbed with work. 'Roughly, I spent nine months of the year working flat out, and three months with the family. From now on,' he said, 'it's going to be the other way round.'

One of the things that has stayed in my mind about Eric Morecambe was his friendliness and kindness to a small boy. Our son Mark, who was at the time ten or eleven years old, had been with me in my office at the BBC when Eric had arrived surrounded by a small company of people. I was never quite sure who they were – management, hospitality, various BBC departmental people? I don't know. I remember only that they seemed to fill the room. Mark, shy and not unnaturally a little overawed, had disappeared behind the forest of grey suits, but not before Eric had spotted him.

'Where's that lad?' he asked. The suits parted to reveal a small boy standing by a desk. 'What's the cricket score, son?'

'I'm sorry,' Mark said, 'I don't know.'

'You know how to get it, don't you?'

Mark shook his head.

'There's a special phone number. If I give you the number, you can make yourself useful and get the cricket score for us. Will you do that?'

Mark nodded.

'Good lad.'

When Mark was dialling the number, the chatter among the grey suits started again. I was touched by Eric Morecambe's awareness of the child in the office and the easy and natural way he had included him in the gathering. When Eric was leaving, he stopped at the door and turned to speak to Mark. He said, 'What football club do you support, son?'

'Middlesborough,' Mark said, without hesitation.

Eric Morecambe shook his head sadly. 'They're going

down,' he said. He winked at Mark and disappeared into the grey suits. The encounter had made Mark's day. It had also told me a lot about Eric Morecambe.

For many performers, the need to maintain a high profile in the pursuit of fame and fortune, in spite of protests to the contrary, becomes addictive, and no opportunity to keep the name 'up front' can be let go, no possibility of a newspaper, radio or television interview can be missed. It is very understandable; in show business, fame is very ephemeral. There are several notable exceptions, musicians and film stars who manage to keep their private lives private and prefer to keep it that way. Curiously, the fact that they are exceptions makes them more intriguing.

Which is probably why I was intrigued by the actor, Keiron Moore. Intrigued because, having secured a place on the film-star ladder, he had changed the direction of his life quite dramatically, to work for the Catholic relief agency, CAFOD. Later, rather than return to movie making, he became an associate editor of the Catholic newspaper, the *Universe*. This was not his first change of direction, either. He had once been a medical student, no doubt with dreams of becoming a doctor. Perhaps the intrigue had a particular appeal to me, because of my own pilgrimage decisions. However, I was to discover that the word 'pilgrim' suggested something far too aesthetic and religious for Keiron's liking. In front of the television cameras he challenged the appropriateness of the word 'pilgrim' in relation to himself. He said, 'Putting the word "pilgrimage" on this whole thing gives some idea that I am good or holy, and I am not. I am the complete opposite. It never looked as if I had done strange things with my life until someone like you came along and said, how did it all happen? The change from medicine to theatre and cinema I don't suppose was an abnormal thing, as I was interested in theatre before I started reading medicine. Frankly, I started to read medicine because I heard you had a good time as a medic, so my leaving university probably means there are a good many people alive who wouldn't have been, had I become a doctor.

'The change from cinema to the Third World is a bigger one, and it probably started way back again. In my middle-to late-twenties, I met a man called Father Michael Hollins who had a profound effect on my life. I was in the church, I had a label, I was a Catholic, I had grown up a Catholic. It didn't mean a great deal to me, but Michael Hollins . . . it wasn't that he preached at me. I was going through a difficult time in many ways. He just happened to be there at the right time and it was because of what he was . . . what he said.

'I'm sure he'd be embarrassed if he heard me say this, I think there was a depth of prayer in the man. He never told me he prayed. There was something in him that somehow made me take another look at Christ and the whole question of the Christian religion. That started a search. The deeper I got in, the more interesting it became.

'I think there's a problem with Christianity, that very often we touch the beginning, but we stay in the nursery. Then, after a time we begin to say, "This is not very interesting. In fact, it's rather boring." It's the one area in our life where we never go in deep enough. What Michael Hollins got me to do was go in deep. It's like skiing; you start on the nursery slopes, but you need to go up the mountain to enjoy it, even if you have terrible moments of panic and danger.'

'Did it seem risky to you, this change of direction – to move into the office of a charity in Soho? After all, you were very successful in your film career.'

'Yes, very strange. Again it was not a decision, it was not the "road to Damascus". I had become interested in the Third World. I had seen poverty when I had been on location in films. I did the usual thing, felt rather guilty when a good location lunch came out for the actors and the crew, and there were children there with very little to eat. One did the sharing bit and all that. Then you went home and said, "That was very sad" and forgot about it. But then I became aware of the Third World as such, and of CAFOD, which is the official Catholic organisation for the Third World. Barbara Ward and Lady Jackson wrote a very good report on what they were doing in self-help projects. This got to me and I began in my own parish to do something about it. Eventually I got to know the administrator, Noel Charles, who is now dead, and he asked me if I would come for six months and help. It was a sabbatical of six months and I did it. It was very dangerous, because it grew. I became more and more involved, then it became a year, two years.'

'Were people chasing you, agents?'

'My agent thought I was a bit mad. Then I suppose he had to suffer that. My background was of some value, because I made a documentary film in Peru. Actually that was a very exciting adventure, because it was on a very low budget. Then I made one in Senegal. But please don't get the impression that it was all gift from my side. I am the most fortunate of men. I have met the most fascinating people. I have been to villages in India. I have shared a meal with Muslims in the north of Senegal. They have welcomed me and shared the little that they had. I have learned a great deal from the Third World.'

'Then you moved, yet again?'

'I was there for about eight years and I began to feel I was getting in a rut in the Third World. I have seen it happen. You just become Third-World-orientated. There are a lot of problems in our own society. At the same time, Rowanne Pascoe, who was editor of the *Universe*, started to whisper about coming to work at the *Universe*, pointing out there were problems in our society and the *Universe* was a paper that was facing up to them. She was bringing about a lot of changes in the paper; she is a most convincing lady when involved in an argument. Then the managing director, Jerry McGuiness, joined in the chorus and once again I saw an opportunity, a form of madness, a new venture, and the search went on, you see.'

'Can you see along the pilgrim path? Can you see the way you might go next?'

'I can't. I would be very foolish to start making predictions about the future. It's those corners. I turn a corner, and find great surprises. I just hope I will keep on searching, asking questions, and that I will end up searching at the right door.'

'In other words, the pilgrimage, even if you don't want to use the word, goes on.'

'It goes on.'

An English Joke

One morning, at breakfast with June, in the restaurant of the Queen's Hotel, I became aware of a man looking across at me from another table. In the early morning, after a good night's sleep, my voice is a bit sepulchral, with the result that at breakfast I am rather inclined to rumble over the porridge and orange juice. When we got up to leave the restaurant, the man from the other table stood up and spoke. His voice had that curious back-of-the-throat whisper, peculiar to Italian operatic tenors, who go to extraordinary lengths to protect their vocal chords when not singing; hence, the whisper.

'Excuse me, please. I must know. You are a singer, yes?'

'Well, no, not a singer,' I rumbled, 'but closely related. I'm an actor.'

'Such a voice,' he whispered dramatically, 'should sing!'

'That's very kind of you, but I expect it's a bit late for me to take up singing now.'

'It is *never* too late!' he said, with that passionate vibrato usually heard only in opera houses. 'There are many wonderful teachers of singing in London. You must sing! Such a voice must sing!'

I learned that he was an Argentine Italian, a tenor playing a guest season with Opera North at the Leeds Opera House.

I was at, that moment, completely unaware that the northern edition of the *TV Times* had, that very morning, printed and delivered to newsagents an edition with a full-page picture of Donald Swann and me, at a grand piano, singing.

The following morning, as we entered the restaurant, the opera singer rushed up to me clutching his copy of the *TV Times*. He thrust it before my eyes, his right forefinger tapping the picture of me, singing with a wide, open mouth. 'I knew,' he hissed, 'that you were a singer! And not only do you sing, but you are a famous singer! You joke with me, yes? An English joke!'

It was very difficult to explain that what I did at the piano, with revue songs, would hardly pass for singing within the confines of an opera house. I fear that he was never entirely convinced that he had not been a victim of the famously strange and subtle British sense of humour.

A Cultural Revolution

One of the curious things about appearing on television is that you rapidly become a recognisable face in the street. You do not actually become famous – real fame comes only after sustained achievement and years of exposure to the public gaze – but after only a few weeks on television you can become what I would call a 'current' face. While this might mean that people you have never met hail you as an old friend, which is not an unpleasant experience, it does not mean that you become rich or that your lifestyle changes to any marked degree.

For a while, you are perceived to be, though you are not in fact, 'different'. Certainly, while your star is in the ascendancy the media world treats you as if you are rich and famous and you begin to lead a dual life, in which in front of the cameras you are a glamorous, media personality, but at home and certainly at the bank nothing has changed significantly.

There are also a great many myths and traditions in the entertainment world, such as the belief that if you have starred in the West End – that is, achieved the ultimate ego-trip of having had your name up in lights in London's theatre-land – you must have 'made it', in every way.

My own experience of this dichotomy of fact and fiction, of make-believe and reality, is probably best illustrated from the time when Donald Swann and I were starring in *Swann With Topping* in the West End, at the Ambassadors Theatre, and we were invited to top the bill in a variety show on television called *Starburst*. We were taken to the television studios in a chauffeur-driven limousine. At the studios we were given the full, star treatment. We had a personal assistant to look after us throughout the day. We had a wonderful dressing-room, food and drink was provided, whenever, we just had to ask. People from the wardrobe department attended to our clothes so that on screen we would look immaculate, and in the studio people from the make-up department cooled the brow and powdered the nose at every opportunity. It was wonderful. It was also wonderful to have our songs accompanied by a full orchestra.

After the recording, the chauffeur-driven limousine had driven us to Donald's house in Battersea, where we had a cup of tea and a chat about the day's work before I went out, saying, 'See you later', and walked around the corner to catch a bus to take me back into central London. Standing at the bus stop, I found myself laughing. The funny side of the situation had suddenly struck me. The day in the golden ballroom was over, the make-believe had finished. Standing at a bus stop in Battersea, this was reality. The facts were that at that time we had only been in the West End for a matter of weeks. We were not, as it happened, earning quite as much as we had been earning in Fringe theatre, and the cheque from our one-off appearance on television would probably not arrive until the end of the month, minus our agent's ten per cent. Somehow, the transition from limousine to bus stop summed up the dichotomy of show-business myth and hard reality perfectly.

Staying in an hotel, when a television company is paying the bill, can also remove or at least cushion and protect you from the sharpness of reality. The main thing is to keep your feet on the ground, to see the funny side of it all, and laugh at yourself a lot. The biggest mistake would be to take the hype and yourself seriously, and to adopt airs and graces based on someone else's money.

One of the most memorable nights at the Queen's Hotel was spent in the company of a man whose feet are planted very firmly in the real world. Yet Jimmy Reid is a man with a vision, a vision as revolutionary as the teachings of the Gospels and very closely related to them.

Not so long ago, in Queen Victoria's reign, there was a very simple work ethic. If you worked hard, you were rewarded. If you didn't work, for whatever reason, you were likely to go hungry. Clearly, in the age of the silicon chip, the work pattern of Western countries can and probably will change dramatically. We've already reached the age of the computerised factory where robot arms and hands can be programmed to carry out machine assembly and construction, to do work that used to be in the hands of a human workforce. In this situation, the Victorian work ethic makes very little sense.

Jimmy Reid was a trade union leader in the seventies. In the shipyards of the upper Clyde he had led a very unusual form of industrial action. Instead of a 'tools down' strike, he had led a 'work in', and the action had resulted in a very satisfactory agreement. He became a kind of Scottish folk hero. He was a popular figure and, perhaps not surprisingly, he was elected Rector of Glasgow University. Eventually his cheerful and original outspokenness led him to being employed as a *Glasgow Herald* columnist.

Originally he had trained as an engineer, but since the days of his apprenticeship the world has changed considerably. I talked to him about the future of work, in the last years of the twentieth century and beyond. I asked him, 'What changes have you seen in work patterns, during your working life?'

He replied, 'There have been profound changes. There has been a whole series of inventions and technological developments that cumulatively amount to the second industrial revolution. I think that is what we are living through. Earlier in this programme you were making references to how, in the modern industrial production cycle, the human hand has been removed, and what has happened is that technology has shifted people away from the actual production process into the preparation of production processes. My attitude lies in the profound belief that we should welcome this revolution as long as we use it for social need and not for private greed.'

I said, 'There is a great fear of technology, isn't there? People fear that they are going to be put out of work because the whole of industry will be changed by some computer system.'

'Not an unreasonable fear. You see, it's not technology that puts people out of work. It's not an advanced technology that does any harm, it's an outmoded sociology. You see, if I could put it this way, if you viewed electricity exclusively from the standpoint of the electric chair, then you'd want to ban it, wouldn't you? But electricity can bring light. It can generate energy. It can bring warmth, or it can electrocute and kill people. How we use electricity is a decision for us to make. This technological revolution should be seen in a positive context. It can liberate people from drudgery, from repetitive work. It can remove people from those industrial areas that are fraught with danger and, of course, you can liberate people from excessive working hours in order to move on to a different concept of living, where we would have to educate our children and ourselves not just for work, but for enjoyment of life, and fulfilment. I think we could, in terms of the new technology, for the first time create the conditions for a new renaissance.'

'A new renaissance? Just supposing that overnight you could say to some people, "You can work two days a week and here's £1,000 for the week", would you do that?'

'Well, let me put it bluntly. If I could negotiate £1,000 a week take-home wage for some workers, at least for a few of them, I would be signing their death certificates because they wouldn't know how to use their lives and time. They would probably drink themselves to death. Now, don't blame them for that. It's not that they are genetically defective in any way. No, the simple truth is that we haven't paid sufficient attention to cultural deprivation in our society.

'We have educated human beings for work. We have to educate them for the creative use of their leisure time. I can envisage a situation in the next twenty or thirty years where the division of labour between the artist and artisan disappears; where everybody chips in, so to speak, to the social good, by doing, say, ten hours of work and then they go away to develop whatever other talents they've got – fishing or golfing or playing music together.'

'A total, cultural revolution.'

'Absolutely, a cultural revolution.'

'Are we actually preparing for that now?'

'No, we are not preparing for it. The point is – we should be. In our lifetime we could achieve a new concept, a new and real vision of culture. Culture isn't the Edinburgh Festival, an esoteric three weeks in the year. The anthropologists' view of culture is of the totality of a civilisation and we, through technology, if we use it for social need, can actually start to create a real culture. Having a cultured existence – it's this idea that people do not recognise, and I'm talking in the labour movement now, because my background is the labour movement. We are very conscious of economic deprivation of the underpaid, but what about cultural deprivation? Millions of working men and women and their children have latent talents which will never find expression. Why can't we use technology, Frank, to liberate that?'

'Just suppose there is a lad who has just left school, he's on the dole. All this talk of renaissance, what does it mean to him? What can he do in his position, as an unemployed youth?'

'It means nothing to him and it means nothing to me unless you're prepared to fight. Now, I don't mean being abrasive and aggressive. I'm for people being on their knees when they're talking to their God, but they should get up off their knees when they are talking to fellow human beings and should demand of politicians that technology and economic forces are not going to dominate human beings, that's to insult us. We are going to control them and use them for our good.'

It's often said that the happiest and most satisfying way of earning a living is to be paid for what you enjoy doing. Quality of life, people say, is far more important than how much you earn. In an ideal world, wealth would be so distributed that no one would need to worry about money, food or clothes. Our chief concern would be the happy and useful development of our individual gifts for the greater joy of the community and ourselves.

I am aware that all this sounds like a Utopian dream. It is a vision that provokes great mirth among the cynical, mirth which is generally accompanied by cries of 'get real!' That, however, is neither a good enough argument nor an acceptable reason for not being committed to holding such a vision before the people of the world and attempting to establish just such a society.

In the theology of the Christian Church, the kingdom of Heaven on earth is a reality, already established by Jesus Christ. The Lord's Supper is a foretaste of the heavenly banquet, taking place in the outposts of the kingdom of God, which are immediately established wherever people gather

in Christ's name, whether they are in Barnet or Buenos Aires,
Canberra or Helsinki. True, the members of that kingdom
are far from perfect, but the love that holds them together is,
and the vision it represents is ever before them.

5 Perchance to Dream

The Good Companions

Getting caught up in the detail of individual performances in particular places sometimes made it difficult to keep one's eye on the end purpose, a run of performances at the Edinburgh Festival Fringe. We had long since completed all the technicalities required to perform at the Edinburgh Festival Fringe, which are in themselves quite demanding. Registration fees had been paid, and details of performances, durations and venues supplied. Securing a venue, or in our case two venues, one for lunch-time and one for evening performances, had not been easy; nevertheless, they had been achieved. The idea was to present our three productions consecutively in the evenings, and at lunch-time to present abridged versions, lasting just under an hour, so that people who worked in Edinburgh and wanted to take in a show during the working day might be able to do so.

The venues looked very promising. The lunch-time performances were to take place at St John's Episcopalian Church which is in Princes Street, in the very heart of Edinburgh, and the evening performances were to be at the Nicolson Square Methodist Church, which is a wonderfully elegant, regency-styled building, lying just off one of the principal roads running into the centre of the city.

We needed to arrange for very large publicity posters to be made, to be posted outside the venues, and also smaller posters and handout leaflets, or flyers. Admission tickets for each performance also had to be made available at the venues and at the Fringe office. 'Strolling' players these days have to be able to organise themselves as well as give the appearance of effortless 'strolling'.

The organisers of the Princes Street venue were not happy about the idea of having a play with a war theme or context, very understandably, because of a previous experience in which a company had presented a production portraying an aspect of the First World War, and the gruelling nature of this production had resulted in a very poor box office. So it was decided that we would alternate the Steinbeck play and the Passion-play at Nicolson Square, and present, also alternately, one-hour versions of *Laughing in My Sleep* and the Passion-play in Princes Street.

Our touring programme was continuing to shape and hone the performances and at the same time establish technical presentations that were highly efficient. *Laughing in My Sleep* was developing into a finely balanced mixture of serious and comedic moments. Pieces were edited, rewritten, dropped altogether, repositioned, reinterpreted. The idea was to construct an entertainment that became a gentle progression towards a clear and recognisable climax – triumphant, preferably. The realisation that we were getting something right came when, after several performances in a variety of places, we began to hear reports of people saying, 'I was laughing uncontrollably', 'My eyes were streaming', 'I haven't laughed so much in years'.

Comedians are frequently insecure about their material and in need of constant reassurance that what they are doing is funny. The actor playing comedy is not quite the same, simply because he is not playing himself, but acting. It is not about asking the audience to love me, so much as loving the character that is being portrayed and the skill of the writer who created the character. In other words, to perform a comic scene from a Charles Dickens' novel is not the same as presenting the 'cutting edge of political satire' or 'telling a joke'.

The Passion-play, for the actor, is a physically demanding performance. In our set-up, the loading and unloading of the vehicle and the rigging and derigging of the equipment, largely supervised and/or carried out by June, makes every production physically demanding for her. While it would be impossible for the actor actually to relive, night after night, the emotional extremes that are conjured up by the play, even the techniques employed to represent those emotions are extremely demanding, physically and mentally.

In Act One there are nine people – each different in voice, character and physique – who appear consecutively before two earlier characters reappear, and the final scene involves the introduction of a tenth character. In the second act, in addition, a further three characters make their entrances. The people from Galilee speak with northern English dialects. Doubting Thomas, for instance, who appears in Act Two and brings a certain amount of light relief to the resurrection stories, is a Liverpudlian Scouser. The people of Jerusalem are West Country, the licentious soldiery are Londoners and Glaswegians. Simon of Cyrene is a foreigner; Cyrene is a thousand miles from Jerusalem, so he is an Eastern European.

The final scene of the Passion-play involves a combination of performance, music and lighting effects which create the impression of someone who just fades away, passes ethereally out of our midst. The timing and coordination of music, lights, voice and action are obviously crucial.

In the village of Emsworth, on the Hampshire coast, where the sea virtually laps the edge of the streets, we reached this final high point and got it exactly right for the first time. Lights and music had faded respectively, the last cried-out words of Christ hung in the air, and in the darkness I left the stage. You could have cut the atmosphere with a knife. It was as if the entire audience was holding its breath. The silence was total and utter. We waited for the applause. It didn't happen.

We gently put up the house lights. The audience still did not move. We didn't know what to do. So I walked back on to the platform and took a bow. And then a sea of applause crashed against the stage. Wonderful! We had got it absolutely right. But the real trick would be to do it again, and again and again.

Chad the Good Samaritan

Fascinating days. In one way, total involvement in theatre productions might seem like living outside of reality, but the real world was all about us as we trundled across England into villages and towns, on motorways, along A-roads, B-roads and even down unclassified roads. Every now and then our political awareness was stimulated by involvement in a television programme and intense conversations about the human condition, like the conversations we had with Chad Varah.

When we stayed at the Queen's Hotel in Leeds we would sometimes dine out with our guests at a nearby Italian restaurant where pizza pastry was made before your eyes, rolled, flattened, stretched, thrown in the air. It was a happy, noisy place with marble tables, a breath of Italy in a Yorkshire city. Chad Varah, the founder of the Samaritans, the telephone befriending service, said that he would quite enjoy an Italian meal so we walked around the corner to Italy.

Rev. Dr Varah, who had once been a staff writer for the *Eagle* comic, was not as I imagined he might be. His name and history suggested someone who might have been slightly Bohemian, so I was surprised to meet a small, bespectacled man in a neat suit with a pocket watch in his waistcoat who, when coffee was about to be served, consulted his watch and announced, 'No coffee for me, thank you. I never drink coffee after eight-thirty.'

One of the most common phrases in the English language is 'Don't worry', which is a lot easier to say than it is to do. In the New Testament, Jesus said, 'Which of you by being anxious can add one cubit to his stature?' St Paul, writing to the Philippians, said, 'Be not anxious about anything.' The fact is, we do become anxious. We become ill with anxiety, develop ulcers, have heart attacks, become deeply depressed. It was awareness of people's anxieties that moved Chad Varah to found the Samaritans. The object was simply to befriend people in distress by listening.

On the television programme I asked Chad, 'Is it possible to define anxiety?'

'Anxiety is a kind of fear. Whereas we use the word "fear" for something immediate and real, like someone pointing a gun at you, we use anxiety for something which isn't immediate, and may not even be real. It may be something you're imagining and that isn't going to happen. A lot of people become very anxious and almost incapacitated because of things which, if they could see them as they really are, wouldn't make them so upset, so worried.'

'What sort of things worry people?'

'It depends on the age group, really. Youngsters worry about their attractiveness and the approval of their peers, students worry about their exams.'

'But those concerns are very natural. They are not the things that you would go to a doctor about.'

'No. I'm not suggesting they were, but if you look at every age group you see there are things that cause a great deal of unnecessary suffering, such as people worrying about the relationships they have with the people closest to them. The middle-aged worry about getting old. The old worry about taking care of themselves. Anxiety about your own health, and for everybody, the anxiety about death coming to yourself or your loved ones.'

'What can people do about those anxieties?'

'Share them. You see, if you can find someone who is sympathetic and will listen patiently to your anxiety, this is a great comfort and often helps get things into proportion, so you stop making mountains out of molehills.'

'Is religion a help?'

'True religion is a help, but many people have false religions that make them more anxious. If your concept of God is someone who is always looking for something to pick on, that isn't going to relieve your anxiety. If you think of God as someone who is watching over you, loving you, caring for you, protecting you, it's a big help. But, of course, you can't give a religion to someone who hasn't got it and if someone hasn't sufficient belief in God to be comforted, then a human voice has to speak in place of God, to speak for God.'

'Of course, there are religious sects that put a great deal of emphasis on a God who is looking down in fearful judgment all the time.'

'Yes, and this is worse than no religion at all. That kind of religion doesn't allow you to live joyfully and tranquilly.'

'But even if you are brought up in a traditional, orthodox, faith, nevertheless you can develop an anxiety about stepping outside the confines of the teaching of your religion,' I said.

'Obviously a person who wasn't at all anxious about whether they were doing right or wrong, living lovingly or unlovingly, would be a very horrid person. We have to have a proper concern about our behaviour. That's a very different thing from anxiety which is crippling. The person who becomes over-anxious is not able to do anything good, or to distinguish between good or bad.'

'I've heard of people who have said, "I have so many problems I don't know where to begin" but, when asked to list their problems, find that in fact they have one or perhaps two.'

'Yes, but the person can only see that having talked to another person. Sharing anxieties is the only way. Of course, some people's anxieties are sufficiently acute for them to need to see a doctor, perhaps. Some people suffer anxieties about going out, or staying in, all sorts of "phobias" as we call them, and they may need treatment.'

'Medical treatment? Taking pills or something to relieve the symptoms?'

'Sometimes treatment is by psychotherapy, that is through counselling, and sometimes medication is used to relieve the state of anxiety. There are medications for almost every state of mind, but many of us think it's better, if you can, to talk it out.'

'If there was someone watching who was anxious, what would you say to that viewer who was worried?'

'I would say don't be alone with it. Find someone you care about, and who cares about you, and share it with that person. If it's so acute that sharing doesn't help, see your doctor. If no one else will listen to you patiently and understandingly, ring the Samaritans. That's what they are there for. You will find that they are there waiting for your call day and night.'

It is a fact worth noting that since the Samaritans were founded the suicide rate in Great Britain has decreased noticeably. Most of us worry too much about the things that have happened in the past or the things we think might happen in the future. St Theresa of Lisieux once said that if she found that she was anxious or depressed, it was nearly always because she had either been living in the past or in the future; when she lived for the present moment, most of her anxieties melted away.

Lord, I've had a curious thought, a paradox.
The more I seek a quiet mind, the more anxious I become.
The more I examine my conscience, the more disturbed I
    become.
The more I try to plan the future, the more worried I
    become.
It seems to be a simple rule, really – anxiety breeds anxiety.

Lord, in your mercy, help me to live in the present, and to
  trust
that as you have led me this far, your guidance will continue.
  Amen.

A Good Life Before Death

When the Methodist Conference was at Leeds, *Laughing in My Sleep* was a conference event. We were rather surprised to hear that the conference organisers had booked the City of Varieties Theatre in Leeds. The City of Varieties is a wonderful theatre, a few hundred years old and used for many years by the BBC to film the Victorian music hall show introduced by Leonard Sachs, *The Good Old Days*. My secret anxiety was related to its size, or rather, the question, would we get a respectably large enough audience to justify booking it?

Walking around an empty and ancient theatre, standing on its stage and looking at the rows and rows of empty seats, you could be forgiven for finding it difficult, in the echoey silence, to imagine that in a few hours' time it would be bursting with people, life and laughter. Anxiety inevitably sits on your shoulder, but it's no good worrying about that, ever. You just have to get on with your preparations, bow to the ghosts of your fellow actors from previous generations hovering in the wings, check your props, go through your lines yet again, and remember not to bump into the furniture.

By contrast with our minimalist theatre equipment, June was now faced with operating a lighting console that probably resembled the flight-deck of Concorde. However, the principle is exactly the same, it's just bigger; and she took it in her stride. A few hours or so before the performance was due to begin, June checked with the conference events desk to see how the tickets had been going. To her amazement, she learned that there were no longer any tickets available. They had all been sold. When the house lights went down and the spotlights came up on the stage-right garden umbrella, I walked on to the stage and looked out towards an audience I could not see, but could hear and smell, and knew that they were packed to roof.

It was one of those nights that imprints itself on the memory for ever. From the enthusiastic burst of welcoming applause, whistles and shouts, through the rapt silences, through the excited buzz and chatter competing with the interval music relayed into the dressing-room intercom, to the final roars of laughter, it was a night to remember. I walked back to the dressing-room. June was already buzzing me on the walkie-talkie. We congratulated each other. Then I sat down in front of the bulb-bespangled mirror and, addressing the actor-ghosts of the dressing-room, said, 'Well, what did you think of the show, fellers?' And immediately, one of the bulbs went out. Make what you will of that.

In the same city, in a television studio, I talked to a remarkable lady, Dame Cecily Saunders. She was so committed to an idea, a vision, that it led her from being a trained nurse to qualify as a doctor in order to pursue her dream. She had a dream of establishing and running a hospice for the elderly and those in a terminal condition. Working for years at the St Christopher Hospice, she devoted herself and her considerable gifts to improving the quality of life of those suffering from incurable illness.

In the television conversation, I got down to basics and asked her, 'Dame Cecily Saunders, what is a hospice?'

'A hospice is a community or a team of people who are concerned both personally and professionally in the quality of life remaining to patients and family who are struggling with mortal or long-term illness giving them pain or other distress, and some are concerned with the frail elderly as well.'

'What do you mean by, "the quality of life remaining"?'

'I mean for many of our people, though not for all, time is short and it matters very much that you fill it up with what needs to be done – perhaps sorting out some of the past, certainly using the present as well as you can. Then thinking about the family and their future.'

'I imagine I would be quite shocked to learn that I had a short time to live. How would I cope with the knowledge that it's short?'

'People usually give you the knowledge bit by bit as you are ready to handle it, as you yourself ask for it. As the Bible says, "As are your days so will your strength be." You don't know how to cope with a crisis until you are in it, but there's a tremendous capacity for using problems and crises, perhaps for doing something at greater depth than you've done before in your life. It's not all loss. It's not all danger you're looking at. It's day-to-day things, often very ordinary, often very amusing. Our job is to control distress or pain, to make it possible for people to use the time themselves and make their own achievements.'

'I imagine you have to be careful how you control pain. If you control it too much, people simply become unconscious.'

'Well, that, we have shown, is not necessary. People are so afraid of some diseases. They associate pain with them and think that pain can't be controlled or, if it is, you are bound to be asleep. What we have been able to show at St Christopher's and other hospices – by our practices, by our research, by our teaching – is that you can be freed from pain and still remain alert and very much yourself. After all, hospices have most of their patients at home, at least as many as in a building, if they have one.'

'If you have patients at home, presumably the patient's family either know, or are helped to learn, how to cope with the illness.'

'Most people have got more courage and common sense than they ever realised. Many find that once they are there, and have some support – and people around who expect them to do well, who also understand some of the difficulties – then they can find it in themselves to do much more than they ever imagined. But don't think that the whole time you are working at that intensity. It's about living life as normally as possible, for as long as possible.'

'Do you have to train people, I mean the family?'

'There's a lot that any community service – the district nurses and doctors and everybody – do, already, in helping families to help their own people. We have some special knowledge, some special confidence and we hope to be able to pass it on. But so often it is we who are learning from the patients, who are learning from the family.'

'Do you mean learning about courage? Learning about coping with pain?'

'Yes, and seeing, over and over again, the particular essence of the individual. I think the heart of caring is attention and respect. It is not that they are poor things and here we are doing something for them. It's they themselves who happen to be in adversity, and adversity for so many people brings out reserves that maybe weren't used before.'

'We have been talking about the specialists at work in the hospice and so on, or people who are directly concerned with illness in their own family. What can ordinary people do to relieve suffering and pain in the world?'

'I don't think you have to look for a special unit. You have to look down the street, step forward, be a good neighbour, to give concern and interest and often very practical support to the people who are either bereaved or in illness or disaster of any kind.'

'Just noticing and doing something about it?'

'Noticing and stepping forward to see what you can do. You don't have to have the good, right words, all prepared. Just let the situation bring it out of you.'

Lord, in that hour, may I think not what I shall say
but know and trust that it will not be me who speaks
but your Holy Spirit speaking through me. Amen.

The Volunteers

Before Malcolm Muggeridge committed himself to the Church, one of his objections to Christianity was that it didn't work. Christians are supposed to love the poor and the needy. 'Why isn't it happening?' he asked.

In answer, a priest said to him, 'But it is happening' and he named Mother Teresa of Calcutta.

Muggeridge immediately came back with argument. 'She is the exception that proves the rule. How sad that there's only one Mother Teresa.'

'You're wrong,' came the reply. 'There are thousands like Mother Teresa. She might be the one who's famous but all over the world there are people living sacrificial lives in the name of Christ.'

There is at least one in every town. The Sue Ryder Foundation is dedicated to the relief of suffering. It's an international charity with its headquarters in Cavendish, Suffolk. It's concerned with the sick and disabled of all age groups, with eighteen homes in this country. June and I visited Sue Ryder in East Anglia. We met again, in front of the cameras.

Her international adventures in care for the needy started at the end of the Second World War in Poland, but I asked when her concern for the needy began and she said,

'As a child, I used to go round deprived areas in the north, visiting with the district nurse and medical practitioners. That was really my introduction to people in need.'

'The need of people in Poland at the end of the war must have been even more devastating than deprived areas of the north of England. How did you become involved with trying to meet the needs of Polish people?'

'I was with the Special Operations Executive (SOE), involved with Polish resistance operations and I ended up in the ruins of Poland at the end of the war. Everything was devastated, acres of rubble.'

'Having worked in the Resistance, you must have been very close to a lot of people.'

'Most of them disappeared or were killed. I was never dropped [from a plane] myself. I didn't really know anyone left from those days. I left the SOE and joined the Resistance as an auxiliary nurse in a medical team that was sent off to organise hospitals in the ruins, which was quite daunting. The temperature in winter would drop to 25 degrees below zero, and the summers were very hot. There was every known, and unknown, disease; TB was rife, and typhoid and typhus.'

'Was it out of this situation that the desire to try to meet the needs, in some way, came to you?'

'Yes. There was a wide spectrum of people, all ages. It was very difficult to make decisions. You couldn't be fair. It was a case of trying to do something for a very large number of people and children. There were homes with domiciliary helpers attached to them. We had some patients being visited in their own houses. Later, we went to other countries in need: Yugoslavia and Italy. We built up the foundation in those countries, and they were eventually taken over by the local authorities and run by them.'

'But your work did not stop there, did it? You moved even further afield.'

'Yes. We moved on to the Third World, where we care for leprosy patients and destitute children. We also build up teams who specialise in preventative medicine, which is just as important.'

'What kind of homes are there in this country in the Sue Ryder Foundation? I know there are eighteen. What do they deal with?'

'Huntington's chorea, which is rather an unknown disease. It affects the body mentally and physically. A devastating disease. There are six thousand known, registered cases in the country and I think the foundation is the only one that offers accommodation and nursing care especially for their condition. The other homes are for patients with rheumatoid arthritis; for young people as well; handicapped children and those in need of psychiatric care; the disabled; those who can't cope any more on their own. Some of our homes are simply for the homeless; and a few are for those with cancer, who need convalescence after surgery, or radium treatment or chemotherapy. Some are in a terminal condition. We have the privilege of being with them and nursing them until they die.'

'Can people volunteer to help? Can young people help in any way?'

'We have quite a lot of volunteers. We always ask for tradesmen with a specific trade, such as carpentry and bricklaying. We need qualified nurses and state enlisted nurses, as well as secretaries, and weekend secretaries for a vast amount of correspondence. Some people give up their holidays to help at headquarters.'

'Do you have young people who go to Poland?'

'Only if they are the tradesmen with special skills to offer. In Third World countries we have to be rather fussy, because the living conditions are very rough, and accommodation and food is scarce.'

'Do they have to offer a particular length of time?'

'Ideally, about a year or two years.'

'Is it fair to say that all this work is inspired by faith? Is it because of your commitment as a Christian that you do this work?'

'Yes, it is. I would never have started without that. I had a very strong example set for me, in the faith of the people I saw in the Polish communities.'

'Do you think that could be said of all the people who work in the homes? Are they all committed in the same way?'

'Many of them are. I can't speak for all of them. Some come from different creeds and backgrounds. The foundation as such is grounded on faith. It ran with no funds at all to start with, just a belief that it was God's will and that everything would work out.'

Every act of love
is a light in a dark world,
a spark of hope
in the midst of doubt and cynicism,
a glimpse of God at work.
It's a strange paradox,
God is love,
and it is God who moves us to love,
and yet whenever we visit the sick,
or feed the hungry,
or do any loving thing,
for anyone in need,
God is loved.
For Jesus said,
'In as much as you did it
to the least of my children
you did it to me.'

The Styx: A Good Crossing

In the year of my ordination, I was sitting one day in the study of my 'father-in-God', Rev. Derrick Greeves.

'Here's a little exercise for you,' he said, handing me a black-backed book, entitled *Minutes of the Methodist Conference*. 'You will observe,' he said, 'that the edition predates the Second World War. If you turn to the section with the page-marker in it you will see a list of obituaries. There are at least ten obituaries there; each records the dedicated life and holy death of a much loved Methodist minister. Each obituary at some stage gives the date of death. See if you can find the actual words "death" or "died" in any of them.'

It didn't take long to see what he was getting at. 'Death' had been swallowed up in euphemisms. No one had actually 'died' as such, but had become engaged in other activities. They had, respectively: 'gone to glory', 'claimed his reward', 'passed on', 'passed away', 'passed over', 'attained the Celestial City', 'entered into a higher service', 'cast his crown before the eternal throne', 'joined the heavenly host' and 'taken his place in the Church triumphant'.

'The euphemisms have now disappeared,' Derrick said, 'but I believe some of our ministers are still very skilled in the art of avoiding the issue of death. One of our responsibilities, as ministers, is to prepare people for death. The best time to do this is not alongside a death-bed, but years before. It is not good enough that our people should reach their last hours and still be asking, "Why me?" or "What's it all about?" Death should be part of our regular teaching programme. Death should be included somewhere in our sermon plan for every year, or as a subject for house groups, or given a session in the annual church retreat. If ministers are afraid to tackle the Christian theology of death as teachers, it is more than likely they have not come to terms with a theology of death for themselves.'

Derrick then spent a considerable time spelling out what he believed and how he came to terms with the difficulties that arose when people came face-to-face with death. A great Pauline scholar, he is now, if you will pardon the euphemism, thoroughly engaged in tackling the great saint about the meaning of some of the more esoteric sayings contained in his epistles. I am therefore unable, as was my practice over the years, to telephone Derrick in order to check that I'd got his theology right. However, I think the following passages are probably pretty close to what he said. I have to say that he was an active man who, if he could talk and walk, was inclined to do so, as he did on this occasion.

'Look, let's just walk down the road, shall we?'

And arm in arm, with only the occasional irrelevancy brought about by the sight of a bus, a person, a dog or anything else that triggered his brain and tongue into comment, he launched into his theme.

'I'm afraid, my dear Dr Topping,' he said. I don't have a

doctorate; that just happened to be one of his favoured forms of address. 'I'm afraid the Church seems to have become somewhat reticent in its preaching about life after death. The idea seems to have developed that we should concentrate on the "here and now" aspect of life, and leave the "here-after" to the hereafter. As a young man, I remember hearing sermons that made the prospect of life after death seem full of excitement. We believed that nothing suffered in this life could diminish the joyful expectations of heaven. I remember sermons in which the preacher evoked images of conversa-tions with ancient heroes and childhood friends and neigh-bours; and vivid images of the communion of saints as a vast fellowship that spanned the centuries.

'It's true that we are living in an age that demands a scientific, "sight, touch and proof" religion. Not content with heavenly imagery, it demands earthly evidence, for it is, my dear professor, "worldly wisdom" that must be satisfied. There's nothing new in this, of course. In the first chapter of the first letter to the Corinthians, Paul speaks about the gospel as "folly to the wise". The Jews demand signs, the Greeks wisdom, but we preach Christ crucified, a stumbling block to the Jews and folly to the Greeks. But to those in Christ that stumbling block and that folly is the power and the wisdom of God, "Because the foolishness of God is wiser than men; and the weakness of God is stronger than men." '

He stopped outside a front garden. 'What an extraordinary rose, beautiful.

'Of course, the entire New Testament doctrine of eternal life,' he continued, 'is alien to the scientific approach to understanding. I'm afraid scientists have so astounded us in this century that some churchmen lean over too far back-wards to accommodate the scientific approach.

'I am not saying that scientists are wrong, but I am saying that a first-class mathematical brain does not necessarily have a right to make theological pronouncements on the basis of mathematical research. I am also saying that if you laid every

scientific discovery, from the beginning of time, at the feet of
the Creator, they would look insignificant when compared
with creation itself. The arrogance of human beings is not
without its humour. It's as if a pipe-smoking, bespectacled
frog, having examined a lock of hair, some nail clippings and
a fingerprint, were to give a dissertation on the mind of the
naturalist, or biologist.

'If we are unable to preach Christ crucified and risen from
the dead, if the resurrection is not true, then we are wasting
our time; we might as well "Eat, drink and be merry, for
tomorrow we die." To live in Christ is to enter the eternal life
here and now. Death is a phase through which we pass in the
process of eternal life. The sooner we can convince our people
that they have already entered the eternal life, the sooner
will death and bereavement become surmountable obstacles
rather than stumbling blocks. I do not mean that the
Christian does not suffer or grieve. Jesus Christ himself wept
for Lazarus. Bereavement is traumatically painful. But
through the love of Christ we know that mourning will cease
and "every tear shall be wiped away". After all, we believe
that,

> Love in Christ puts death to flight,
> love prepares the place
> where love, with love will all unite
> before that loving face.

'Look here, all this theorising and poetry is well enough,
but let's get down to some of the practicalities of ministry to
the bereaved. You don't wear aftershave, do you?'

'No. I don't shave.'

'No, of course you don't.' He kicked a stone along the
path. 'Symptoms. There are all kinds of signs and symptoms
to be looked for in those suffering grief. We have to minister
to the whole person – not only their spiritual difficulties, but
also their physical and material problems. Death is always a

shock for the family, whether or not the death was sudden or long-expected. The actual moment of separation is deeply disturbing.

'We mustn't be deceived by outward appearances. People frequently present a facade which may well be the exact opposite of their true feelings. Calm cheerfulness may hide deep depression. Sullen and demanding behaviour may mask a desperate need for affection. Many people develop an unjustifiable sense of guilt, and spend an excessive amount of time brooding on "If only I had done this, or that".

'Loneliness is a major contribution to depression in the bereaved. The older person frequently has few, if any, contemporaries left and is dependent on the younger generation for visits. In middle age, loneliness can also be acute. People are embarrassed by death and bereavement. They do not know what to do, or what to say to a friend in grief. They are not being deliberately unkind, but out of embarrassment they avoid what might be an uncomfortable meeting. So a youngish woman who was once socially active within a group of couples is suddenly cut off by the death of her husband. She is not visited by her old friends. She is not invited to people's homes and she herself feels incapable of rebuilding a social life.'

He pointed at a tree. 'My brother, Trevor, did a rather good watercolour of that when he was last down here.' He shoved both hands deep into his overcoat pockets. 'You see, the single person who has spent many years looking after an elderly relative is frequently quite numbed by the emptiness of her days. Although, actually, in time there is usually a sense of release, and a realisation that a completely new life has become possible.

'Children can be deeply disturbed, if only because adults are afraid to tell them the truth. Those who send their children away until the funeral is over deprive them of a valuable, emotionally maturing experience. Children need to share in the family's emotional upheaval. If children are not sent away they are often silenced or discounted on the grounds that they are "too young to understand", when in fact their spontaneous reactions and assessments are often able to clarify the confused mind of the adult.

'The reality of death should not be hidden from children. That kind of deprivation is more likely to harm than protect. By sharing in the family experience they are drawn closer to other members of the family. Children need to grieve, but they will be able to accept the reality of death far better if they are allowed to share in the family's grief rather than be protected and shielded from it.'

He looked at me as if he had just remembered something. 'Have your children had any experience of grief?'

'Well, in a way, yes. Pets. They held their own, quite solemn funeral service when their guinea-pig died. She was called Lily the Pink, so they sang the song, 'Lily the Pink', when they stood around the grave at the bottom of the garden.'

He nodded with all the gravity associated with adult counselling of the bereaved. 'Children are far more resilient than we allow. They have the capacity to understand and accept the naturalness of death. However, they must be supported by a lot of love and reassurance from the family; otherwise the death of a close relative can be extremely disturbing. Of course, in a previous century, with large families and a high infant mortality rate children used to grow up accustomed to the idea of death being part of life. Nowadays, people can be quite mature adults before they have any personal experience of death.

'It's the whole family, you see. We have to be aware of the whole family, not only at the time of the bereavement but also in the long days and weeks in which the bereaved struggle to come to terms with their loss. We must visit the bereaved, talk with them, listen to them and pray with them. We must be prepared to give them time. A "quick" visit may salve the conscience, but it gives the bereaved no opportunity to unburden themselves.

'You can't do it all yourself you know, but church members have an important ministry to offer the bereaved. A visit from a friend from church, or a member of a church fellowship, will be greatly appreciated. Their visit, however, must not be substituted for a visit from the minister. People do expect their ministers to be ministers, to bring the word of God to their situation. It is a fearsome responsibility which we cannot, ultimately, delegate. We are so often with people in moments of crisis. It's the nature of our calling. We share these experiences throughout all the years of our ministry.'

He laughed. 'You are very patient,' he said. 'You've been a probationer minister for three years now, and I'm teaching my granny to suck eggs.'

'No, you are not,' I said. 'I've spent most of my time with students. I'm quite inexperienced really.'

'Perhaps so, but I think you are probably already aware that as our experience increases, we begin to notice patterns of behaviour. As we become accustomed to grief, we acquire a rather specialised knowledge.'

Suddenly, he became intensely interested in a small ads board hanging in a newsagent's shop window. 'You can't pretend to minister to people, you know. You have to be genuinely concerned. Concerned enough to want to help practically as well as spiritually. A few well-chosen prayers are not enough; you have to minister to the whole person. I mentioned "guilt", didn't I?'

'Er, no, I don't think you did.'

'Well, the most common guilt is to do with feeling that you have not done enough, that you have neglected the person who has died. Then there is the guilt associated with unhappy memories – of heated or unkind words, past moments of conflict. There is a tendency to relive these moments, as if the survivor is trying to punish himself for his guilt. None of this is particularly healthy. In fact, it can quite easily become a self-indulgent exercise that becomes a bit of a habit. It's surprising how much energy can be expended in self-pity. Your job, of course, is to try, gently, to redirect it into something more positive.

'Hostility towards doctors and nurses is not an unusual reaction, with all those embittered, soul-destroying attempts to attribute blame. You know the kind of thing I mean. "He would have been alive today if . . ." "It's gross negligence . . ." Sometimes the bereaved is filled with a desire to take legal action. This is almost invariably an unwise, unhealthy and unhelpful exercise which can only hurt. For anyone to enter into litigation while emotionally disturbed by grief is something that is best avoided. Hostility coupled with guilt and very expensive legal charges can be extremely dangerous. The hostility can turn inwards, you know, and can lead to despair, even suicide.'

He stopped walking and seemed to look at me intently but was, I think, thinking rather than staring. 'Didn't you have a student who committed suicide?'

'No. I stayed up all night with a young man who had talked about suicide.'

'It's not true, you know.'

'What isn't?'

'That people who threaten suicide don't do it.'

'Yes, I know. Your brother Fred said so in a psychology lecture in Bristol.'

'Did he really?'

I nodded, 'Yes.'

We walked on again, his mind back on the subject of bereavement. 'Grief does funny things to people, you know. Sometimes there is an obsession with the memory of the person who has died which amounts almost to an inability to accept what has happened. They tell you things like, "We've kept his room exactly as it was when he was alive". Or they set his place at table; though this often happens accidentally, from long habit, absent-mindedly. "Seeing" her face in a crowd, "hearing" his voice in company. These are fairly common signs of inability to come to terms with the fact of death. Although, I suppose most common, and most of all to be expected, is the feeling of "distance" from other people; restlessness, aimlessness, inability to complete simple tasks or even sentences.

'So, what can we do? Not a lot immediately. We can visit, listen and talk with patience. When they are ready for it, and you need the wisdom of Solomon to know when that is, we can encourage them to come to terms with their experience and to make a life for themselves. People often say, "I will never be the same again; I feel as though half of me has died." In a sense they are right; they will never be the same again. There is no cure for grief. They have been deeply wounded in the battle. However, wounds can heal; they may leave a scar, but in time we can learn to live with them.

'It might sound obvious, but people vary enormously in their ability to cope with bereavement. One can hardly work out a timetable for grief but, if it does not seem too clinical to say so, I think that usually, in the case of someone losing their lifetime partner it takes about two years for people to *begin* to be able to live with their loss, or as people often say "to feel *normal* again".

'If there is no attempt to overcome the depression of grief, then deep morbidity will develop. In elderly people in particular it can mean the loss of the will to live and, as people used to say, they can "die of a broken heart".

'Do remember that people who have been through a similar experience can be helpful, and are often very willing to help you out when it comes to visiting. When you are visiting the bereaved, be prepared to give a bit more time than usual. Sometimes people need to reminisce, to remember old times. You may be asked questions about life after death. They will not want, nor be able to take, a sermon. They may not be able to concentrate on anything you say, but they may still need very straightforward reassurances, simply expressed, about things they already believe. You have to give those reassurances by talking about your own faith in the promises of Christ.

'Oh, look! There's Nancy with the laughing eyes. I think it's time for a cup of coffee, don't you?'

'We believe in life before death', the Christian Aid slogan, must surely be one of the best and most positive slogans ever adopted by any organisation. It cheers me whenever I see it. At the same time, it does not absolve us from tackling the issues directly related to the business of death and dying.

A few years ago I received a letter from a lady who was in her nineties. She wanted me to visit her and talk about death, and life after death because, as she said, 'Nobody will talk to me seriously about dying. The local church people are very kind. They visit me, and so does the vicar, but whenever I ask the vicar to talk about death, he just becomes very jolly and says things like, "Oh, you don't want to worry about that, my dear. You'll outlive me. Now, what about a nice cup of tea and another of those wonderful scones." So, will you please come and talk to me about dying, and life after death?'

It turned out that she lived only a mile or so away from the home of my parents-in-law, in Hampshire. So I found I could do as she asked, on one of our family visits. I told her what I believed, but she did not want convincing. She did not enter into argument of any depth. She just wanted someone to take her questions seriously; perhaps most of all she wanted to share, with someone else, her belief that her own death would be a 'staging post' in an ongoing pilgrimage.

Television viewers of a certain age will remember the drama series, *Dr Findlay's Casebook*, and they will remember the actress Barbara Mullen, who played Janet, Dr Cameron's housekeeper. I had the privilege of working with her for a few months, and on one occasion she had told me that she had been with her father when he had died. I said, 'Oh, how sad.'

But she had said, 'No, it wasn't. Not at all. It was a beautiful experience.'

Apparently he had asked for her, and when she was sitting beside his bed he asked her to sing for him, which she often did. On this occasion, when she had finished singing, he said, 'Now, don't be afraid. I will have to go soon, but not far. It's just like going into another room.'

She sang to him again and while she was singing he looked up at her and said, 'It's just the next room' and then he went.

'It was beautiful,' she said. 'It was as if, in the words of the famous spiritual, he had seen that sweet chariot, "coming for to carry him home".'

Of course, faith in the resurrected life is not only a great comfort to people facing death but it can also be a source of strength that keeps us going at other times. Rev. Vernon Stone became a prisoner of Chinese revolutionaries when the Communists took power in China. He was kept in solitary confinement, except for interrogations, which always seemed to happen in the middle of the night. He told me that what kept him going was the Easter story, and the knowledge that his faith was centred on Christ who had conquered both sin and death. He felt that no matter what they did to him they couldn't take away the risen Christ from him. Even if they took his life he would still be with Christ.

A Good Lord on a Soapbox

One of my guests on the Yorkshire Television programme was Lord Soper. I had asked him if he would talk specifically about 'life after death'. I began the conversation by asking, 'Lord Soper, what would you say to the argument that life after death is merely a pleasant dream invented to comfort the bereaved?'

He replied, 'I would want to begin, I think, by saying of course it is a dream, but then dreams have a great relevance to reality. It is a comfort, but I believe it's rooted in a reasonable supposition, quite apart from the evidence that we see of the resurrection of Jesus Christ.

'The more scientists are apparently able to plumb this extraordinary universe, the more certain they are that the old materialistic concept really won't work and the spiritual reality of life is not confined to, or shut into, a material framework. There is no ultimate reason why, when the body no longer is a function or an expression of the spirit, that the spirit itself withers with the body.

'That, so to speak, is the suppositional argument, but the other most powerful argument, to my thinking, is that people want it. We have an innate confidence in the idea of life after death, and that thinking belongs to, and I use the old word, the "ontological" argument. The very fact that we are here, looking for something beyond, is prime evidence that we aren't mistaken.'

I had to take my hat off to Donald Soper. I wondered if I would be throwing my version of the ontological argument into a television discussion when I was in my eighties. I said to him, 'It's very difficult for people to actually conceive of life after death, even to think of it. When I was a child we were told that we had souls. I imagined a soul to be some white amorphous thing which, when I did bad things, got spots on it, and when I was very bad it went black all over. Every now and then if I did something good it got wiped clean. When I died, it was this white amorphous thing that went to heaven.'

Soper smiled and said, 'If you are asking, "Have we got souls?" it rather depends on which way you look at life. A materialist, in very large measure, looks at matter, material reality. If you look at it from another aspect, for instance, when you are listening to great music, you are considering a more spiritual reality. We are souls *and* we are bodies. The inference I draw, that has comforted and reassured me over the years, is that the more you trust in the evidence of the spiritual reality of life, the more questions fall into their proper place, and the more answers you seem to get.'

I said, 'For some people, the idea of existing for ever is frightening.'

'I don't know much about the next world,' Soper said, 'and I'm always a bit suspicious about those who do. They seem to know more about the next world than they know about this. I would take my comfort, not in the assumption that you can specify how it's going to look, nor what you are going to do. The questions are innumerable. No, I prefer to take the position Jesus took, when he was asked about it, "In my Father's house there are many rooms, if it were not so I would have told you. I go to prepare a place for you."

'I think the greatest element in belief, and confidence in life after death, is not to try to work out what it is going to be like, but if you believe God is your heavenly Father, who cares for you in this world, then you have every right to believe that if you love him and serve him here, then all will be well.'

'St Paul,' I said, 'tried, in a way, to explain his vision of resurrection life when he talked about not having "earthly bodies" but having, in the resurrected life, "spiritual bodies".'

Lord Soper said, 'Of course Paul was afflicted by this bug of rationality, part of his Greek background, I suppose. There's a lot of Greek thought in the Acts of the Apostles, not only in his own writings or his own letters, and I think it's a waste of time, I really do. I find a great many people who are putting on their hat and coat for the next world are better employed rolling up their sleeves in this.'

'What about the resurrection accounts?' I asked. 'How convincing are they?'

'I am very glad that those resurrection accounts do not tally. If they did, somebody would have been cheating. When my answer, as a schoolboy, was completely and absolutely the same as the boy next to me, there was an enquiry. What happens in the resurrection is that they were so certain that their friend had come back to them that they gave their own accounts of it. There are accounts of football matches which don't tally, but you don't doubt that these matches took place.

'It is the very simplicity of the attitude of those who wrote these stories. You see, you can't explain the fact that a number of frightened, disheartened men and women, within three days, are beginning to turn the world upside down. You don't make that up, and then be prepared to die for it. It was the fact that their friend came back to them which is the immutable fact of history as I see it.'

Out of the corner of my eye I saw the studio floor manager give me the 'half-a-minute' sign, so I put my final question. 'If you had one single statement to make about life after death, what would it be?'

'I think I would want to say that life after death is the experience of Jesus Christ, which begins here and is immortal in the sense that nothing that can happen on this planet, *nothing* – not even death – can destroy it.'

Risen, But Not Yet Fully Ascended – Pardon?

Oswaldtwistle Civic Theatre is, in its own way, a name with which to conjure. It was once a town hall, in its day of glory, until changing borough boundaries altered its status. However, it has risen from the ashes to find new life as a theatre serving the adjacent communities of Accrington and Burnley. I'm not quite sure what it is about the word 'Oswaldtwistle' that makes one smile. Perhaps it's because it suggests an archetypal Lancashire mill town, with women in shawls and flat-capped men in clogs talking about 'Arkwright' and 'trouble at t'mill'. It provoked some mild amusement on BBC Radio 2, when Terry Wogan enquired about our current bookings. When I said we were about to play Oswaldtwistle Civic Theatre, he had said, 'Oswaldtwistle? Oswaldtwistle Civic Theatre? You certainly know how to hit the high spots!

There's no stopping this man! Oswaldtwistle today. Tomorrow, the world!'

In fact, it was one of the high spots of the tour. The invitation to perform in Oswaldtwistle had come from a Methodist minister, Rev. Wilf Green. When I heard that he had booked a civic theatre, I wondered if he might possibly have bitten off more than we could chew. Would he be able to gather an audience from his churches big enough to justify booking a civic theatre? I had not allowed for his natural skills as an entrepreneur. He had not only advertised it in more than one Methodist circuit but he had booked and arranged coach parties. In the event, Oswaldtwistle Civic Theatre was bursting at the seams.

The theme of our play, *An Impossible God*, is nothing less than 'the Passion, death and resurrection of Jesus Christ'. Not surprisingly, it opens up a whole raft of highly debatable and contentious ideas.

After the Oswaldtwistle Civic Theatre, we drove east once again, making for Leeds and the Yorkshire Television studios. Sometime back we had passed Brighouse, famous in our family for its great and triumphantly successful brass band, the Brighouse and Rastrick. I was recalling a brass band competition I had once attended in Wigan when June said, 'Was the idea of resurrection from the dead a new idea? Was it introduced by Christianity?'

'No,' I said, dragging myself back, mentally, from Wigan. 'I think the idea of resurrection has been disputed for thousands of years. It was a contentious issue before Jesus Christ was born. The Greeks had a doctrine of the immortality of the soul, which is not quite the same as the idea of resurrection. Resurrection is, of course, still disputed in our own sophisticated age but, significantly, it was hotly disputed during Christ's own lifetime. In fact the Gospels record part of one such dispute in which Jesus himself was involved.

'Jesus was in the Temple, in Jerusalem, being questioned

about the resurrection of the dead and he said, "Have you not read what was said to you by God? 'I am the God of Abraham, the God of Isaac and the God of Jacob.' He is not the God of the dead, but of the living." And when they heard it, they were astonished at his teaching.

'People are still astonished, and still life after death is doubted, disputed and denied. But Jesus did not only teach with words, he taught with his life. He preached love and lived it. He declared truth and demonstrated it. He promised resurrection and his wounded feet walked to Emmaus and his pierced hands broke bread. His promises about life after death were unequivocal, "I go to prepare a place for you. If it were not so, I would have told you."

'For those who believe in Christ's promise, their faith is a wonderful source of courage, energy and joy. Listen to the conviction and joy in these words written by the late Canon Henry Scott Holland:

> Death is nothing at all. I have only slipped into the next room. I am I, and you are you; whatever we were to each other that are we still. Call me by my old familiar name; speak to me in the easy way in which you always used; put no difference into your tone; wear no forced air of solemnity or sorrow. Laugh as we always laughed at the little jokes we enjoyed together. Play – smile – think of me – pray for me. Let my name be ever the household name it was. Let it be spoken without effect, without the ghost of a shadow in it; life means all that it ever meant; it is the same as it ever was. There is absolutely unbroken continuity. What is this death but a negligible accident? Why should I be out of mind because I'm out of sight? I'm just waiting for you. For an interval, somewhere very near, just around the corner. All is well.'

June said, 'Who was the chap who wrote a book about

resurrection? He was a monk or a religious of some kind. You met him in Bristol.'

'Oh yes, that was Harry Williams, H. A. Williams, an academic religious. He used to be a fellow and lecturer in theology at Trinity College, Cambridge, but gave it up to become a Mirfield priest.'

'Mirfield?'

'Mirfield in Yorkshire. It's the headquarters of an Anglican community called the Community of the Resurrection, oddly enough. The book he wrote was called *True Resurrection*. My old friend and colleague, Peter Firth, invited me to join him and Harry Williams for lunch in the BBC canteen in Bristol, when the book came out. That must have been in the seventies when I was with BBC Radio Bristol. It is a wonderful book.

'He said that there are "resurrection" experiences to be found in the lives of many people. He gave the example of a marriage that has begun to go dry and stale, in that the couple were now merely going through the external observances of marriage but without the richness and excitement and commitment that they had once known. Then a new relationship begins to emerge – perhaps not as wild and passionate as in the past but deeper, more stable, more satisfying – a rediscovery of each other, finding a new life in each other that is not dependent on constantly recharging emotional batteries. This newly discovered relationship, he said, is resurrection. When people's hopes are destroyed and yet from the wreckage of their dreams a new vision emerges, this is resurrection. When, out of the catastrophe of a premature death, the bereaved person finds new depth and meaning and new and different purpose, this is resurrection.

'Harry Williams saw these new beginnings as the resurrecting activity of the Holy Spirit. Whether it was in the form of a fresh start in a struggling marriage, or starting a new job after redundancy, in such new beginnings he saw resurrection. Put like that, it's possible for all of us to consider making a fresh spiritual start, to contemplate inviting the Holy Spirit to lead us into resurrected life, now. Of course, every new beginning holds an element of risk. You could say that God took a risk in the incarnation of Christ, but that the risk was necessary to give the human race the opportunity of making a new beginning.'

We had pulled into that part of the railway station car park reserved for the Queen's Hotel's guests. The Queen's was originally a railway hotel. June said, 'The Harry Williams idea is OK, in a poetic kind of way. But what about actual resurrection? What about the idea of continued existence after death? What did Jesus say about that?'

'Well, Jesus did speak directly about our resurrection and his own. In John, referring to the "temple" of his own body, he said, "This temple will be destroyed and in three days I will rebuild it," and perhaps the best-known of all his teachings on the subject is, "In my Father's house are many mansions." As I said earlier, there is that unequivocal saying, "I go to prepare a place for you, so that where I am you may be also. If it were not so I would have told you." His words to the thief on the cross also ring with authority and conviction. "This day, you will be with me in Paradise." Not, "I pray that . . ." or "I hope that . . ." but plainly and powerfully, "This day you *will* be with me in Paradise . . ."'

We lifted our cases out of the car, put the steering-wheel clamp in place and then activated the central locking.

'To be fair to Harry Williams, the "new beginnings in everyday life" concept of "resurrection" is only a small part of his book. He also explores many other aspects, including physical death and resurrection. Though "resurrection life" this side of the grave is also present in the teachings of Jesus. For instance, there is resurrection in the story of the prodigal son. It is the story of a young man whose life has collapsed in ruins, but in his decision to return to his father lies the seeds of resurrection, the possibility once again of new life. The whole of the Christian life can be seen as a journey to God, just as John Bunyan envisaged it in *Pilgrim's Progress*. Many of us have started on this pilgrimage, and perhaps lost our way; some of us may have even given up; but Harry Williams's message, and the gospel message is, it's never too late to start again. A new beginning is always possible on the ultimate pilgrimage, and the ultimate pilgrimage is the one that takes us into the mystery of true and eternal resurrection.

'I think one has to say that even the closest followers of Jesus, the apostles, did not appear to understand that his messianic mission was about revealing the resurrecting action of the love of God that enables the human race to defeat both sin and death.

'In the story of the transfiguration, Jesus tells Peter, James and John not to tell anyone what they have seen, "until the Son of man has risen from death." They obey him, but the Gospel says they started discussing among themselves, "What does this 'rising from death' mean?" They appeared at that time to have no understanding, and certainly no expectation, of resurrection.

'Judas's betrayal, it is thought by some, was not a lack of faith in Jesus, or a terrible mercenary cynicism, but in fact an action meant to precipitate the messianic purpose that he believed Jesus could achieve; that is an uprising that would free Israel from the yoke of the Roman Empire. He had recognised the messianic power of Jesus but had completely misinterpreted it. His suicide was the despair of someone who had failed utterly to understand who Jesus really was, and the real purpose of his mission.

'I heard an Oxbridge professor say that if the story of the resurrection had emerged in the last fifty years of the twentieth century, no one would have believed it. What the professor did not appear to appreciate was that when the events of Christ's death and resurrection were reported two thousand years ago, nobody believed it then.

'The first people to reject the idea of the resurrection of Jesus Christ were not sophisticated academics, but the people who had been closest to Jesus. The first people to say they did not believe were the apostles. When Mary Magdalene ran to the upper room and announced that she had seen the risen Christ, they did not believe her. She runs with a message for them, given to her directly by Jesus, and what happens? Some dismiss it as "an idle tale", and others, more kindly, put it down to "a woman's grief". You can imagine the comments, can't you?'

June smiled and said, 'Oh, yes. I've heard them.' She slid into a brief kaleidoscope of voices and faces that started with Mrs Gamp, touched on Thora Hird and ended with a character that I suspect began life in the mind of Victoria Wood. 'Does stra-aange fings to people, grief. Some people, I do believe, Gawd bless 'em, jus' can't take in the – ve'ality – of deff, can they, my dear? And what about our Elsie? Talk about lost! She was still setting Arnold's place at the table a month after he was six foot under. Poor old soul. She's never been the same. Start imagining – don't they? Start "seeing" things – don't they? Shame really, i'n't it?'

We had walked into the street and were approaching the rather grand front entrance when I said, 'You know, for centuries we have referred to Thomas as "Doubting" Thomas. "Doubting" sounds as if he were not quite certain, doesn't it? What he actually said, however, were not words of "gentle" doubt. They were the angry words of a man who knew what death was. He was a down-to-earth realist. He knew that the only kind of body they took down from a cross was a dead body. He did not want people to mess about with his emotions with talk about Jesus being "alive". His protest against the claims of his friends was a violent, even vicious attack on what he saw as intolerable irrationality. "When I can put my finger in the holes in his hands, and in his side, *then* – I'll believe!" is a quite horrible thing to say. It was meant to shake them out of their unrealistic reverie. So the apostles were very far from being starry-eyed believers. Yet almost every one of these "unbelievers" died as martyrs, refusing to deny their personal experience of the risen Christ, including Thomas.'

We signed in at the Queen's Hotel reception desk and made for the lifts. Staring up at the illuminated numbers which seemed to indicate that the lift had come to a permanent rest on the fourth floor, June said, 'So, something very convincing happened to them. But what?'

The lift nearest the restaurant had started to move. I was still considering June's question when the lift doors opened and what appeared to be a Nigerian chieftain in national costume and his wife, who was wearing a headdress that would only just pass under the door, stood staring at us in apparent amazement. I smiled, and was rewarded with smiles that would undoubtedly bring out the sun in Leeds or Lagos. We stepped aside and they made a majestic entrance into the hotel lobby.

As the lift grumbled its way back up to the fourth floor I said, 'You know, I think the New Testament is largely a collection of people's failures to describe what they experienced.'

The lift clattered to a halt, and the doors slid open to reveal an echo of Queen Victoria's glory on the fourth floor of the Queen's Hotel. June said, 'That has to be sweeping generalisation.'

'Of course it is, I'm just trying to make a point. You see, the problem is, how do you put into words something that no one has ever experienced before? Some pretty rum things happened in those days, and when they tried to describe them, one can only say that words failed them. After all, they were not poets or philosophers, they were fishermen and carpenters, working men and women. And even if they had been gifted writers, still, how would they find words to describe something which no one had ever seen or witnessed or experienced before?'

'With difficulty?' June suggested, helpfully.

'Exactly!' I said. 'Take whatever it was that happened up

Mount Tabor, or was it Mount Hermon? Actually, I think they call it the Mount of Transfiguration these days. Anyway, something happened that defied description. They said that his face "shone like the sun" and his garments became whiter than it was possible to wash any garment. Afterwards, they did not speak about their experience to anyone. No doubt they didn't, because if they had, people would probably have thought them mad.

'Take the story of Pentecost. In the accounts of this event, people said that there was a sound "like unto" a mighty wind, which filled the entire house. It wasn't a wind but it was a noise "like" a wind. There was no report of any damage, but the noise filled the inside of the house. And then they saw what looked like tongues of fire, which touched the heads of everyone in the room. Looked like, but were not, in fact, tongues of fire. Speaking as one who served his time as an altar boy, in the days when the only Mass celebrated in the Roman Catholic Church was the Tridentine Latin Mass, I can tell you, I know what happens when flame touches hair. Whatever they saw, it was not flame as we veteran altar boys know it.'

In our rooms, suitcases had been deposited on those curious webbing devices for holding suitcases, coats hung on theft-proof wardrobe hangers, a kettle was working itself up to boiling point and I was standing looking down on the noble statues that guard the triangular 'square' that faces the Queen's Hotel.

'Tridentine Latin Mass?' June said, without the slightest trace of weariness in her voice.

'A Mass that conforms to the rules of the Council of Trent.'

She smiled sweetly. 'The Council of Trent?' she said, like someone pushing a button on a multi-choice, automatic, railway-ticket vending machine.

'A council that tried to steady the Roman Catholic boat after the rocking it had received from the Reformation.

Anyway, to get back to Pentecost, and tongues of fire and all that, I think all these passages are attempts to put into words events that were not only material events but also spiritual experiences, and how do you put a spiritual experience into words? Those who met the risen Christ were attempting to describe events that actually happened to them as material, historic events, but were also, at the same time, deeply spiritual experiences which virtually defy description. When you experience something that has never been experienced before, there are no words to describe it. If and when you try, it might not make sense to those who have had no similar experience.

'Mary Magdalene struggles to explain her experience. She sees Jesus, speaks to him, yet fails to recognise the man who had changed her entire life. He speaks her name and suddenly, as if scales had been lifted from her eyes, she recognises him. It is almost as if she has been "allowed" to recognise him. I remember reading a commentary that had a wonderful phrase that said it is only "the eye illuminated by faith" which can penetrate through the passing reality of the physical world to the unchanging reality of the spiritual.

'Anyway, Mary then moves towards him, embraces him, but Jesus says, "Don't hold on to me. I am not yet fully risen." What on earth, or in heaven, did that mean? I wonder if Mary's response to that was, "Pardon?" I can't imagine that it was crystal clear to her what he meant. Did it mean that his resurrection had created a new relationship between them; not now physical as she had known it yet, yet still personal? Did it mean that he was in a state of transition, that it was necessary for her to recognise him, but when he had "ascended" the physical would be transcended, by a form of relationship that is outside our current experience and understanding? However Mary understood it, her first words to the disciples were, "I have seen the Lord." Whatever else she understood, she understood and believed that. She knew she had spoken to the risen Christ.'

'Are we having dinner with Bob Champion tonight?' June asked, dragging me back to twentieth-century Leeds.

'Er, I don't know. I'd better check with reception, and see if there are any messages from the studio.'

From the Ashes of Disaster

The jockey, Bob Champion, made a remarkable recovery from cancer. After a series of quite gruelling chemotherapy treatments in the early days of the development of this method of attacking cancer, he not only recovered but began to ride again and eventually rode in the Grand National and won it. He is an excellent example of Harry Williams's idea of 'resurrection now'.

In the Yorkshire Television studios I asked him to tell me his story. I said to him, 'Bob, you are looking very fit now, but when was it that you learned that you had got cancer?'

'It was in the summer of 1979. I was riding in America at the time. I spoke to medical people over there and they suggested I came back to England a little bit quick.'

'That must have been a pretty terrifying experience.'

'I was petrified when the doctors told me I would have to have operations. After I had the operations I started a course of chemotherapy, which in the end went into six courses. I must admit, I was petrified.'

'Because you thought that cancer meant the end?'

'Well, all I had read was of people dying of it. You rarely heard of people recovering from it, yet a big percentage of people do.'

'The treatment itself – at that time it was quite severe, wasn't it?'

'Yes, it was very hard on people. Luckily enough, with all the tests and experiments they are doing it's getting a lot easier. They are using different drugs with a better success rate.'

'Reading your book, it appears there were one or two occasions when it seemed to me that you almost gave up?'

'Yes, I did have some bad times. Once I was determined to give up and the nurses said, "Have a walk round the hospital, and have a think about it." So, I did. I walked through the children's ward and saw a lot of little children in the same boat as myself and they weren't making any fuss about it, and I thought "Why should I?" So, I went back until the treatment had finished.'

'Did you have any aims that helped you at that time?'

'Yes. I wanted to get back to riding the National. It got to be a bit of an obsession. I wanted to get back and win the National and, luckily enough, it all came off.'

'This must have been entirely in your head, because surely other trainers and owners must have doubted whether you would ever *ride* again, let alone ride in the National.'

'I think most people did, but they kept giving me hope and that bit of hope from other people made my obsession grow even more.'

'Your obsession to ride in the National again?'

'First of all, to *ride* in the National, and then to *win* it. As I got nearer, I very definitely wanted to win it.'

'Was there a time before the National when you saw that the possibility was strong?'

'Yes, when the horse came back and won at Ascot, the Whitbread trial there. I really thought that if I jumped round, whatever went in front of me would win.'

'Were you sure of your ride?'

'Yes, I knew he would win.'

'When you came out of hospital it must have been difficult to get rides of any kind, mustn't it?'

'I went to America because I thought the pressure would be a little easier over there. Here I was being hounded by the press and everybody saying, "Is he fit?" or "isn't he fit?" I rode for about three months out there and I'd ridden a few winners, so it was easier then, when I came back here.'

'Were you actually fit? Did it frighten you getting back on a horse again?'

'The first time in a race, I was petrified. When I got down to the gate I thought, "Am I going to let people down?" But luckily I won.'

'Did you find difficulty with muscles?'

'I did when I first started riding work, but the more work I rode, the better it got every day.'

'The other thing I found remarkable was the forecast that you would lose about a third of your lung capacity, but you seem to have made a complete recovery.'

'Yes, I have, but it was very hard work. I used to go running every day, and I played squash and tennis and it seems to have come back gradually.'

'The thought of the National always ahead of you.'

'Yes. I used the National as a goal. I think everyone needs a goal in life.'

'You go back to hospital even now, I believe.'

'Yes. When I go back for my tests, or when I'm driving by, I usually pop in and see the nurses and doctors, and they always say, "Would you come and see so-and-so because they've just started the treatment and give them a little bit of hope", and I just hope I do.'

'You go and talk to the patients?'

'Yes, because they don't know what to expect. You don't feel too bad before the chemotherapy starts, but after two days, you don't feel too good.'

'Of course, the side effects can be quite frightening, and quite depressing as well.'

'I think the worse thing, mentally, is that you lose all the hair off your body. Maybe I'm very vain, but it was the worst part of the treatment for me. I don't know why because, really, it's the easiest bit. Your hair grows back. I suppose you doubt it coming back, but I'm now 100 per cent fit.'

'You've had to work at the breathing, muscle control and everything. That must require a lot of effort and courage.'

'Yes, I think when you start trying to get fit after the treatment, you've got no muscles on your body. You feel very weak and so you have to start all over again.'

'Was there a time, during the Grand National, when you thought it was possible that you might win it?'

'There was a time, about 100 yards from the winning post, when I was sure I'd win it. It was just a great thrill. You can't explain what you feel, you just have to have done it.'

'If someone came to you now, and said, "I've got to go through chemotherapy", what would you say to them?'

'I would say, "Start as soon as possible, because you've got a very good chance of full recovery." It really is worth doing.'

'Even if they are not going to win the Grand National they can start a new life. Of course, not only were you aiming to win the National, but you dreamed of all the other things a young man hopes for, marriage and a family. Those things were in your mind as well, weren't they?'

'Yes, especially the family. When I was told I had to have chemotherapy I was told that it was very doubtful that I would have children, but luckily the treatment was very new and they weren't sure about it. Well, last year we had a little boy, so everything has come right.'

Start All Over Again

Throughout Christ's ministry, he challenged and called people to new beginnings, a new way of life. Simon, James and John left their nets to follow him. Paul was called upon to do a complete about-turn. Ever since the days of the apostles, men and women have come to realise through experience that it is never too late to make a fresh start. It might require a great deal of faith and courage, or it might be the realisation that the life you have – any life – is a bonus, that you have known such disaster that now all of life is 'resurrection' life.

I met Alexandra Connor on the *Five Minute Show*. She had been the victim of a brutal assault, in which she had nearly died, just yards from her Kensington flat. I asked her what the experience had done to her life. She said, 'It changed it dramatically, because months after it, I began to paint. That's what happened. I had to have an operation, I had to leave my home and everything. So it changed the whole emphasis of my life.

'I didn't want to go to art school, because I didn't want to be as good as a contemporary painter, or as good as my peers. I was looking at Velazquez or Caravaggio. I thought, "If you're going to go for it, girl, really go for it, set your sights." I had all the time, because of the situation I was in. I'd lost everything, and I had to find something to consume me, and there is nothing that consumes better than art.

'You get lucky people who are born with some special talent, like athletes, and most of them go through life without losing anything. But I think, inevitably, they come to a time in their lives when they meet a situation they have never met before, and they find it more difficult than us normal people, who end up failing and getting up, and failing and getting up again. It's so easy when things go well. You just carry on and you don't think about things. When things go badly, you say, "Hang on. Why is this thing taking place?"'

'It wasn't merely a hobby, was it? You became professional. You made a living doing it.'

'It took me three years and about nine hundred ruined canvasses and that cost money. Believe me, if you make a mistake you don't do it again. You have to pay for it. When I finally got my confidence up and started, I did some work for the Royal Shakespeare Company – in fact, portraits for them – which was very nice. I got commissions after that and I exhibited in Asprey's in Bond Street and then went on to other galleries in London.'

'You went from that to writing novels. Another discipline again, a totally different discipline. What was driving you?'

'I get bored easily. That's the trouble. I always have done. I need a lot of stimulus constantly. I need a lot of change. I could never give up the painting and the writing, because everything is different. Every painting is different. Every portrait is different. I do allegorical paintings which are very, very complex and take months to paint. That is your world, totally. It is your way of seeing.

'It was the same way with the writing as it was with painting. I was poorly. I read a book. It was not Balzac, just a middle-of-the-road sort of book. And I thought, "Hey! I could do this." So I wrote a book and sent it off to these publishers, who said, "Thanks, but no thanks", basically, but, "We like your style, come in and see us."'

'You say, "So I wrote a book." It takes eternity to write a book, doesn't it?'

'It does and it doesn't. I never think. I have this terrible self-confidence, and I also think, "Sod it. What's the worse that can happen? I can fail." The worst had already happened to me, Frank. I had nearly died. If someone looks at me and says, "I don't like your painting, I don't like your books", so what? They are not going to take me outside and strangle me again. That is where disaster can be very, very valuable for people. That is something I'd like to put over: the fact that there is a tremendous advantage. You come up a hell of a sight tougher than you ever believed.'

Alexandra Connor did not use the word 'resurrection', but I cannot think of anyone who, through terrible disaster, found a more completely new way of life.

6 Out! Out! Damned Spot!

Who, Me?

Guilt and forgiveness are closely related subjects, if not inextricably linked. In successive television programmes I spoke to two very different people about the difficulties of coming to terms with guilt and forgiveness. It's almost impossible to discuss either of these subjects in a completely objective manner, simply because everyone's understanding of them is related in some way to their own experience.

How well do you know yourself? Of course, it's very difficult to see ourselves as others see us. A lot of actors can't watch films of themselves. Some people can't bear to have their photograph taken, and a common reaction for people hearing themselves on a tape recorder for the first time is, 'That cannot be me!' Confronting ourselves is very difficult. The most difficult aspects of mistakes and failures are recognising our own guilt and forgiving ourselves or accepting forgiveness. Sometimes we feel that our failure is too terrible to forgive. The idea that someone might wipe the slate clean to enable us to start again seems almost too much to hope for; yet that is exactly what Christ offers when he says, 'Your sins are forgiven you.'

T. Dan Smith had held a position of responsibility in the community as an elected councillor. After two major trials in which he was found 'not guilty' of a number of charges involving the misuse of funds, in a further trial, he decided to plead 'guilty', and was sentenced to imprisonment for six years.

Despite having been a councillor, used to arguing his corner, in the television programme he did not find it easy to articulate his thoughts on what was clearly still a very sensitive and vulnerable area of his mind. Yet, in our conversations in the dressing-rooms and in the studio, his internal struggle to come to terms with his awareness and understanding of guilt did emerge. Sometimes his silences were more eloquent than his words.

I began our studio conversation by asking, 'Dan, fortunately, few of us, having to face the truth about ourselves, end up having to spend six years in prison. What did it mean to you to be sent down for six years?'

'The shock of going to prison is a traumatic experience . . . Six years is a long time. You are cut off from your family, and you know the morning headlines are going to scream all the worst things about you . . . It's traumatic, and it fills you with despair . . . But, the decision having been taken . . . by yourself . . . to plead guilty . . . you've had time to adjust to it. You know you've come to a critical time in your life, but you are not aware, at that stage . . . just how critical a point you've reached.' He seemed to be reliving the events in his struggle to find the right words.

I said, 'That must have been the start of one kind of suffering. But there must also have been a different kind of suffering before that.'

'Yes. I had already had . . . almost four and a half years of suffering, because I had had two trials before that . . . critical ones in the Old Bailey and the Strand, which I had won. So, having, if you like, convinced juries, then . . . to take a decision . . . by yourself . . . to plead guilty . . . is a big step. And waiting, for the trial and the evidence collecting . . . You can't go anywhere, you can't go out, you can't go to sleep . . . it follows you, wherever you go . . . into a kind of despair. It certainly . . . undermines you . . . and of course, you see your family suffering with you, which is even more difficult to cope with.'

'There was a moment then, when you actually came to terms, by your own standards, with the idea that you were guilty?'

'That's right . . . yes . . . I think it's important for people to understand . . . what it is to look at yourself . . . and decide . . . to be guilty. I learned that day, and subsequently in my life, that so often . . . I had been the judge . . . who had decided that I was innocent. If I was rushing out of a morning and I couldn't find my wallet, I'd say to my wife, "Look, if you hadn't asked me to get the milk, I wouldn't have lost my wallet." That's a minor incident, but it's typical of the way you judge yourself as always being in the right. After my pleading guilty, and going to prison, I rarely rush into judgments. I think about it. Now I would say to my wife, "I've lost my wallet. Would you help me to find it?" . . . I think the decision to accept the guilt was a good lesson that I learned at that time.'

'Not to attribute blame immediately to someone else?'

'That's right. When you go to prison . . . the one thing you have in common with the other prisoners . . . you're all guilty. I pleaded guilty, and I was guilty. Many of the men contended that they weren't guilty . . . but you are all prisoners. You move into an environment . . . where . . . you see people suffering in the extreme, and if you have . . . come to grips with yourself . . . you somehow feel you are in a position to co-operate . . . understand others . . . and to form judgments, because you have been judged, yourself, in that you have said to the world, "I'm pleading guilty. I'm not asking a jury to judge me." I think the experience I had, of pleading guilty, of being a Category 'A' prisoner, is a very important step. Once you've gone inside, you are with people who are suffering intensely. You are alongside them and they accept you as one of them . . . because you've said you're guilty . . . and they take your word for it.'

'In order to maintain your sanity,' I said, 'you wrote poetry about what you felt, the agony of the isolation. There's a little poem to a seagull, in which you talk about standing on tiptoe to look out, at that uncaged bird, at its freedom; and here is Homo sapiens, incarcerated, caged, in this way.'

'There are two points I would like to make. You've got to escape. After a while they allowed radios in prison, in my time, and Radio 4 used to get me up to music which is one of my great loves. The other thing is . . . you have to come to terms with the reality of prison. I was called out to assist in a situation . . . where a man had committed suicide. That's another reason why you have to stand away from it . . . because you can't live . . . constantly . . . in those extreme circumstances and survive. That's the reason why you want to escape and look at the world outside. You want to escape from the world inside, yet still feel compassion, still want to help people . . . who get into that . . . despairing position, and many of them will . . . in prisons . . . tonight.'

'Would you say that your ability to feel compassion for others is the result of facing the truth about yourself?'

'Yes, without a doubt. If I hadn't accepted . . . that I was guilty, I would be among those who keep saying, "I shouldn't be in here." It hasn't got anything to do with moral or legal evidence. The evidence in the press is irrelevant to you. You know that the press will make the worst of it . . . or the best, from their point of view. No matter what the evidence, if I have looked at myself, and the circumstances make me say . . . I feel guilty, then I will plead guilty. I can take it on from there. I'm in a better position to judge . . . to try to make amends, if that is the right way to put it.'

'Is there one single truth that you would like society to face?'

'Yes. I think it's the idea of justice with compassion and . . . if anyone is making a judgment . . . and you don't have the evidence, and you rarely have . . . start off with com-

passion, give some benefit of doubt and then . . . hesitate to
make a judgment.'

Forgiveness, Legally Speaking . . .

The guest in the next programme was Lord Denning. There
was a fifties Flanders and Swann song, which referred to the
'Denning Report' about national security, so the name existed
in my mind like a name from history. I never imagined that I
would actually meet Lord Denning, but then I never dreamed
I would meet Michael Flanders or go into partnership with
Donald Swann.

Lord Denning was 85 when I met him at the Queen's
Hotel in Leeds – a bright-eyed, smiling man, with a
wonderfully warm Hampshire voice. I remember his age
because it was his birthday the day we met. We had asked the
hotel to put some birthday flowers in his room, and his
birthday party was the evening meal with June and me.

He did not drink and he didn't drive – not, he said, for
puritanical, moralistic or 'green' reasons, but because they
were both areas of vulnerability. So many lives had been
shattered and careers ruined as a result of errors of judgment
in both those activities. He had made the conscious decision,
as far as it was possible, to reduce the possibility of his being
involved or responsible in either of those areas of possible
tragedy.

At the dining-table, which I seem to remember the hotel
staff had kindly decorated with some celebratory candles, we
talked about concepts of forgiveness, from government
amnesties to divine forgiveness. It was good, rich conversation, full of stories, debate and humour.

In the morning, June, who had taken on the honorary role
of hostess to the television programme's guests, drove Lord
Denning to the studio. I had left for the studio earlier. In the
hotel car park, Lord Denning had some difficulty in locating

the seat-belt locking device, and he said to June, 'Oh, I'll just hold it across.' June had smiled and said, 'It's all right, let me do it for you' and she had snapped the buckle shut. In those days, the driver was responsible for the passenger's wearing of seat belts, and it had crossed June's mind that she would not want to have been held responsible for an unbelted passenger who was a retired Law Lord.

It has been said that the most difficult thing to do is to forgive yourself, or to stop blaming yourself. People seem to have a varied understanding of what forgiveness means. For instance Queen Elizabeth I once said, 'God forgive you – but I never can', which seems a long way from Christ's reply when he was asked, 'How often must I forgive someone? Should it be seven times?' Jesus had said, 'Not seven times, but seventy times seven.' And from the cross, Jesus had pleaded on behalf of those who persecuted him, 'Father, forgive them, they know not what they do.'

Real forgiveness involves reconciliation. In marriage, we don't merely recognise each other's faults but, in love, we learn to live with them. That's forgiveness, and love. Others may desert us, but those who love us stand by us, no matter what we may have done. Love and law are not mutually exclusive, but in some ways they are not natural bedfellows, or are they? Who would know better than someone who had spent nearly forty years on the bench and twenty years as Master of the Rolls.

My first question to Tom Denning was, 'Lord Denning, is there any place for forgiveness in the law?'

'Certainly, in many branches of the law. I have had to deal with it myself, particularly in family law, husband and wife, and also in criminal law, when a man has committed a crime and the question is whether he is to be treated leniently or forgiven.

'Perhaps that which I've been most connected with is husband and wife. Take the ordinary, almost too ordinary case, where a husband goes off with another woman, or a woman goes off with another man and then, there's a chance of reconciliation, and the one who's gone away repents and seeks to come back. Should the innocent one forgive or not?

'Well there, I would say, there is a touch of the divine. If the injured party says, "I forgive you. Come back", that is not only human forgiveness; I think that is a touch of the divine forgiveness.'

'Would a lawyer's training,' I asked, 'include trying to encourage such an idea of forgiveness?'

'When there's a chance of reconciliation, I would hope that all lawyers would do everything they could to help for a reconciliation, for the support of marriage. I've always said that marriage is the foundation, and a firm family relationship is the foundation of our civilisation.'

'What about the judge,' I asked, 'who has to find a person guilty, or when a person is found guilty and the judge has to pass sentence? Can he show forgiveness in the sentencing?'

'He can show mercy. And in a way he can show forgiveness. Now mercy – let me tell you about a case, ages ago. I was trying a criminal case where a man – I don't think he'd had too much to drink – was driving recklessly or dangerously. He went right across the road and killed two innocent little girls on bicycles, and he was charged before me with manslaughter, or causing death by dangerous driving.

'What should I do? He was very sorry indeed. He repented his mistake. The parents of the girls wouldn't forgive him. In a sense, I did. I showed mercy; I only sentenced him to nine months. Perhaps it was too lenient, but I was showing mercy and in a sense I was forgiving him. I don't know whether I was right or wrong. But a judge is often called upon, if need be, to show forgiveness.'

'Would you say there was, in law anyway, an unforgivable sin?'

'Yes, in a sense. But I think you can always show mercy except – well, take murder. Of course, I'm old enough to have sentenced people to death; I've tried people for capital offences. If a person was guilty of murder so far as the judge was concerned, there was no place for forgiveness. The sentence of the law was capital punishment, usually hanging by the neck until death, and the chaplain after that said, "And may the Lord have mercy on your soul."

'No. There is no place there for the judge to offer forgiveness. Whether there would be for the Home Secretary is another thing. No, there are some crimes in which forgiveness, so far as the judge is concerned, plays no part.'

'So I suppose, really, that the difference between divine forgiveness and human forgiveness is that the only condition required of God, is that we turn to him and repent.'

'Certainly. So far as human forgiveness is concerned, in the husband-and-wife cases I told you about, it was always conditional, but if a person offended again, the offence would revive. So human forgiveness is often conditional on good behaviour in the future. Divine forgiveness, I would like to think, is complete and absolute; the sin is wiped off the slate altogether. God's divine forgiveness makes us hope (we all commit sins), we hope that perhaps we shall be forgiven.'

'Do you think it will be difficult – is it difficult for a judge to accept forgiveness for himself?'

'Yes. I think so. I don't know whether other people are like me, but there are some things I could never forgive myself for, and I think other people are the same. There are some things you regret, and you can never forgive yourself. I don't know whether God will.

'Even though you're a clergyman, there must be lots of things you can't forgive yourself for, I should imagine. I've got dozens I can't forgive myself for, and I don't know whether I shall be forgiven in the future. I don't think any ordinary person forgives himself. You ask forgiveness from others, and hope that God will forgive us our sins in due course.'

Lord Denning clearly had a difficulty with the idea of forgiving yourself, saying repeatedly, 'How can you forgive yourself?' It might be worth considering this. If God forgives you, then who are you to withhold forgiveness from yourself?

Forgiveness is an expression of love, and the forgiveness of God is the love that takes away the burden of guilt. If we can accept that love and that forgiveness, then our burden can be lifted, because the love of God not only forgives, but also heals and restores, which is perhaps what human law should do also.

Veni, Vidi, Venues

Our little travelling theatre company could be described as 'minimalist', in that we carry the minimum amount of equipment required in order to create a theatre in whatever town or village, church or hall, we find ourselves.

People sometimes ask, 'How do you cope with all that travelling? All the loading and unloading, setting up the equipment, taking it down, driving on to another town, where do you get the energy?'

The answer, quite simply, is, 'We love it!' If you love what you are doing, you do not even think of it as work. We love every aspect of it, from the telephone call or letter confirming a booking, to planning the travelling, doing the lighting plot, meeting people and performing. Every time we start the engine, we are setting off on an adventure. Last Christmas, I was at a dinner where one of my table companions was the BBC Radio 2 presenter, John Dunn. He confessed that he was, to a certain extent, envious of the 'Good Companions' aspect of our way of life and invited me on to his radio show to discuss it.

If we are going to a place which is new to us, we go prepared for, and anticipating, the challenge of coping with whatever size or shape of space that is presented to us. Some time before the event, we send our advance literature and information pack which includes posters, a programme that can be photocopied and technical requirements, such as the size of the space in which we would like to work, and a request that where it is possible, a 'platform' be provided. Most churches and church halls do not have raked auditoriums and therefore it is quite important for the acting area to be raised a little.

So far we have not been defeated by the shape or size of the space offered. We have worked on a stage set up across the angle of an 'L' shaped room, so that the performer had to be aware of the fact that there were two audiences viewing the play from different angles, but somehow it worked. If the day in question is going to include a long car drive, the setting up of lighting and sound equipment and the performance of a full-length play, we would probably rather not want to be involved in the construction of the platform. But, when it comes to it, you take it in your stride, and it becomes just another part of life's rich tapestry. Everywhere we go, we meet people who are kind and helpful and generous and fun, and it is amazing how much kindness and laughter make work not only lighter but even desirable.

The venues vary enormously, as do the performance areas. Once, in a particularly huge and galleried Methodist church, we had to set up on a specially constructed platform that was just below the level of a gallery and required a ladder to get on to it. It is not easy to make a dramatic entrance up a ladder so, eventually we devised a set of steps to create a 'style' over the balcony rail, which made getting on to the platform a lot easier. My only concern then was to make sure that I did not fall off the platform, which, with scene changes happening in blackouts, was quite a possibility.

Falling off makeshift platforms, while holding a certain comic potential, is also quite a serious consideration for the strolling player. I remember a scene in a W. C. Fields movie in which he fell off a stage and when a woman asked, 'Are you hurt?', he replied, 'No, Madam. I had the great presence of mind to land on my head.'

June usually puts broad strips of white gaffer tape round all the danger points to help prevent disaster. I have only ever once come off a platform which fortunately was only about two foot high, and I was back up again so quickly that afterwards, talking to various people, it seemed that nobody had actually noticed that I had been off and back on again. Or perhaps they were just too polite to say.

Good, well-planned lighting is crucial when it comes to creating a dramatic atmosphere. For the minimalist theatre company, a well-designed lighting plot can compensate for a lack of scenery, or even act as a total substitute for scenery, because through focusing on particular areas, with a sharp edged 'spot', or an interesting colour, it is possible to concentrate attention on the essence of a scene or a speech and draw people, intimately, into the life and world of the people who inhabit the play.

On with the motley!

7   Out of the Depths, I Cry;
Lord, Hear My Prayer

Doing Prayer

It was through our friend Joan Martin that I got to know
Rev. J. Neville Ward, the author of several lovely, but
sometimes demanding, books on prayer and spirituality, the
best-known of which are *Five for Sorrow, Ten for Joy*, a study
of the fifteen 'mysteries' or themes for meditation used in
the Roman Catholic devotion, known as the rosary, and also
The Use of Praying, which is a book for all who would wish to
grow in the life of prayer.

I had met Neville when I had been a student in Bristol
and he a minister in Bath. We enjoyed, of course, the
collegiality of both being Methodist ministers, but it was
only when the three of us – Joan, Neville and myself – met
up in London that we began to get to know each other. We
had gone to see a French film written and directed by Eric
Rohmer, called *Ma Nuit chez Maud (My Night with Maud)*,
which despite the racy title was in fact an intellectual
conversation that continued through a very long night.
One film review described it as, 'a subdued, literate talk-
piece which finally exhausts rather than stimulates', though
curiously enough Eric Rohmer was nominated for an
Academy Award for this film, as a writer in the 'best foreign
film' category.

Years later, Neville retired to Canterbury, where I visited
him when I was a school chaplain in Kent. I drove down to

Canterbury with another friend and colleague, the Reverend Norman Wallwork, among other things, in order to thank Neville for the very generous review he had given, in the *Church Times*, of my book, *An Impossible God*. I thought he had been especially generous, perhaps because of our friendship, and implied as much, when I visited him.

'Oh, no,' he said. 'Friends usually come off worse. You have to be rigorously critical of a friend's work in order to escape the sort of criticism you've just implied. No, I meant every word.' He clearly did, as I was to discover not long after this conversation.

A broadcast I made for the BBC Radio 4 arts programme, *Kaleidoscope*, came about directly through Neville Ward's review of my book. I had a telephone call one day from a BBC producer asking if I would present a criticism of the theology of the libretto of Handel's *Messiah*. Intrigued, I asked who had put him on to me.

The producer said, 'The Reverend Neville Ward. I telephoned him asking if he would do this theological review of the *Messiah*, and he had said, 'Oh, no, not me. You've got the wrong chap. I'm "prayer"; Topping is "Passion".'

Neville died a few years ago, but whenever I meet up with Joan Martin, Neville and *Ma Nuit chez Maud* is always triggered in my memory.

Over the years, I've become more and more convinced that prayer is a way of life. It's not so much the use of 'words of prayer' as an attitude to living and breathing. It's a way of seeing, hearing, and thinking, of 'being', I suppose. It's a way of living which involves what the seventeenth-century Carmelite, Brother Lawrence, called the 'practice of the presence of God'.

There is, of course, a great treasury of traditional prayers which have been used down through the centuries, but in our work-a-day, multi-media, open-plan offices, or travelling on trains with built-in cell-phone neighbours, or in the familiar growl of our hoot and horn grid-locked traffic jams, it's not so easy to recall these ancient prayers, unless we are very familiar with them. So in the rush of these turn-of-the-millennium years, how is it possible to introduce a spiritual dimension to our lives? The prayer contained in John Greenleaf Whittier's hymn, 'Dear Lord and Father of mankind', has never been more appropriate.

> *Drop thy still dews of quietness,*
> *Till all our strivings cease:*
> *Take from our souls the strain and stress,*
> *And let our ordered lives confess*
> *The beauty of thy peace.*

Three days after visiting Rickmansworth once again, we had checked into the Queen's Hotel in Leeds. The guest on the programme was to be the retired Archbishop of York, Dr Stuart Blanche. The subject was prayer. Immediately before the discussion, the Leeds Parish Choir sang the hymn, 'Angel voices ever singing', which poses the question, 'Can we know that thou art near us, and can hear us?'

I took my first question from the hymn and asked Dr Blanche, 'Can we know that God is near?'

'I think so. Even as a child, long before I had any formal instruction in the Christian faith, I think I was aware of the presence of God, although perhaps I would not have given it that name. I was brought up on a farm in Gloucestershire, surrounded by all that loveliness. I still remember thinking how lovely it was, feeling a certain sense of gratitude to someone who was above and beyond us all.

I have certainly had times since, in the Air Force, and at other times . . . I'm afraid in times of crisis, you are marvellously aware of the presence of God. Of course, you can't live your life on the basis of occasional experiences or crises. I take my stand for that on the promise of our Lord himself, who clearly believed in the presence of God with him, and tried to teach his disciples to expect the same. Therefore, yes, in the sense that we know anything, I think it is possible to know, by faith in our Lord, himself.'

'Supposing we accept that God is nearby, what,' I asked, 'can we expect from our prayers? I mean, does prayer work?'

'In my own case, I have to say it works. I wouldn't be sitting here, I wouldn't have survived without prayer. So, in a sense, I am still alive, due to the fact that I have found that prayer has worked in my own life. Like everyone else, I've had times of stress and difficulty and in those times I learned to let go, and wait. Listening, I discovered spiritual resources for life, which I would not have had otherwise.'

'Some people think of prayer simply as asking for things – "Dear God, can I have £200, by Monday morning, please?"'

Dr Blanche grinned, 'I've sometimes done that, I must say, but I wouldn't regard that as the most serious aspect of prayer.'

'And I presume that if you don't get your £200 on Monday morning, you don't say that prayer doesn't work.'

'I think, really,' said Dr Blanche, 'that prayer is a relationship with a person, like a relationship with a human father. If you are constantly asking for things, that is only a very tiny part of the relationship. It's a relationship of trust and security, a way of life, really, not just an activity.'

'Most people's lives,' I suggested, 'are busy and involved with surviving, and most people find it difficult to pray. One imagines a clergyman to have much more time. Is that in fact true?'

'No, it isn't. I think I would have to say that it is more difficult. I have found my prayer life, and the time for quiet, more difficult to provide for as an ordained man than I ever did as a layman. I began to pray, as a layman, in the Air Force. I took it seriously and set aside a definite time in the morning and the evening, even under those conditions, which were pretty rough and difficult. But it is equally difficult in my life now to be sure of making time in the morning, and having some time early on in the evening before the engagements start, when I can do just that; when I can sit, relax, wait and listen in the presence of God.'

'Do you have any methods, any "signposts" throughout the day that help you to pray?'

'I've always tried to do that. I was helped by being given one of those watches which goes "peep" at the hour and "peep-peep" at the half-hour. Well,' he grinned again, 'that's almost a help, except that I don't always hear it now. Nevertheless, anything like that is a help. Think of different things every time the telephone rings, or every time the clock strikes in the church tower, or every time you go to the door. I think these things, you have to work out your own, they are an enormous help in realising again the presence that you have already experienced in your set times of prayer.'

'I find the little prayers easiest, like Lord Astley's before the battle of Edghill, in which he said, "Lord, thou knowest I will be very busy today. If I forget thee do not thou forget me." Do you have any prayers that you go back to frequently?'

'In a way, yes, although sometimes I engage the good Lord in what you might call honest, homely conversation, you know – "you'll have to get me out of this one or you'll have to see me through this one." These are scarcely prayers in the traditional sense. One, which often quietens my mind, and that's the important thing, is that marvellous prayer – I can't remember who wrote it,

> *Lord, temper with tranquillity – my manifold activity,*
> *that I may do my work for thee with very great simplicity.*

'That really does represent a prayer of the heart as far as I'm concerned.'

Rendezvous

When we left the studio, June and I set our faces in the

direction of the Peak District for a short period of retreat –
not a religious retreat, just a break to 'compose ourselves'.
Some years ago, a friend told me about her mother who,
every day, at some point in the day sits down, closes her eyes,
takes a few deep breaths and then with her eyes closed,
assumes a beatific smile and goes into what appears to be a
coma. She started doing it when the children were small.
When the children first noticed what she was doing they had
asked, 'Are you all right, Mother?'

And she had replied, without opening her eyes, 'I'm just
composing myself, my darlings.'

It became a family joke. 'Where's Mother?'

'Oh, she's just composing herself.'

It may have seemed funny to the children, but almost any
parent will recognise and sympathise with her need. Our
going off to the Peak District was intended to be one of the
ways in which we might compose ourselves.

We have gradually built up a list of places that combine a
sense of being 'away from it all' and also provide us with a
sense of security. One of the difficulties of travelling around
the country in a vehicle stuffed full of technical gear is that
you are very vulnerable to thieves. We have had the vehicle
broken into and now, as a general rule, we try never to leave
the car overnight in an insecure place. If necessary, we will
unload every single item and take it indoors, rather than leave
it in a public car park, or anywhere where there is easy public
access to the vehicle. It's a Volvo Estate that has now clocked
up close to a quarter of a million miles. The places we enjoy,
not just for security but because we like them, are farm-
houses. Bed and breakfast on a farm is usually not wildly
expensive and you are nearly always parked well off the road,
in a barn or in an enclosed yard with lots of nice farm dogs,
with their supersonic hearing and hypersensitive nostrils,
who would raise the whole neighbourhood if a stranger put a
toe over the threshold at some suspicious hour.

Driving along the A6 towards Peak Forest, in the High

Peak of the National Park. I reflected on how much I was looking forward to meeting the rest of our family: our children, our son-in-law, daughters-in-law and grand-children. Every now and then we plan a gathering of the clan and arrange a family rendezvous. Sometimes we rent a house; it could be in the UK, it has been in France a couple of times, once we virtually took over a small coaching-inn hotel in Wiltshire. However, on this occasion, the rendezvous was at one of the farms where June and I often stay.

One of the rules of these gatherings is that nobody need feel compelled to do anything. If there is a move to go to a fair, walk up a hill, go into town or swim in a river, everyone is free to do whatever they want. The only thing we definitely do together is plan, cook and eat the evening meal which lasts most of the night, because it progresses into singing, telling stories and playing games that we have invented over the years, but the day is your own. It doesn't mean you don't do things together; it just means you don't have to. I had decided that after my conversation with Stuart Blanche one of the things I wanted to do, on my own, was to spend an hour putting into some kind of order my thoughts and experiences about prayer and spirituality. Decisions were made about who was doing what with whom, and who was responsible for what, in the evening meal. Walking boots clumped in the yard, engines started, and the laughter and shouting suddenly ceased.

I started to scribble.

Prescription Prayers and Crystal Castles

People who have devoted their lives to exploring prayer and spirituality seem to divide prayer initially into two forms: meditation and contemplation. In spiritual terms, 'medita-tion' is when we pursue an idea or a religious question down various avenues and express our thoughts in words as we go along. We do this in an act of worship when we examine our consciences and say prayers of confession, or when we count our blessings in prayers of thanksgiving, and when we gather together our concerns, and list the things that trouble us in our prayers of petition and intercession. The psalms are the meditations of men and women coping with tribal nomadic life nearly three thousand years ago, but they touch on such universal human experiences that they speak to every age that reads them.

Gathering our thoughts together like this can be both calming and restorative. Dr William James, a Victorian medical practitioner, once wrote, 'The exercise of prayer in those who habitually exert it must be regarded by us doctors as the most adequate and normal of all the pacifiers of the mind and calmers of the nerves.' He did not, of course, say that prayer would necessarily cure illness or even reduce pain, but to find even a measure of peace and calm must contribute towards health and in many, many cases it is an important contributory factor towards recovery. The study of human psychology, even now, is still in its infancy, but it is acknowledged that a huge area of physical illness and human suffering has psychological root causes.

From time to time, I am asked if I believe in healing. Do I believe that there are people who have a healing gift? My immediate answer is yes, and to say that I have been blessed by an experience of healing, but second, I would have to add that I have reservations. First, my experience of healers – that is, people who have an actual healing gift – is that they are generally quiet people, not given to displays of loud and dramatic appeals to the Almighty but then, Jesus himself was a quiet healer. Whether the healers have healing in their voices or in their hands, both are usually administered without drama or noise. I suspect that when healing services are worked up into people shouting and writhing and rolling about, even if healing is being administered, something else is going on that has more to do with the healer's needs than those who come for healing.

If we take Jesus as our example, we are aware that he was concerned with wholeness; that is, not simply physical but spiritual well-being. To be 'whole' is to be spiritually, emotionally and as physically healthy as our bodies allow. What Jesus offered people was forgiveness, reconciliation and the love of God, all of which were healing. At the heart of a great deal of illness is the inability to forgive and to accept forgiveness. That deep-seated need for reconciliation may be so well hidden and so deep that people are unaware of the cause and ask for treatment only for the symptoms.

In the Lord's Prayer, there is a phrase that has a condition attached to it. It is the only part of the prayer that is conditional. It's the phrase, 'Forgive us our sins' and the condition is, 'as we forgive those who sin against us'. It's significant, I think, that Jesus once healed by saying, 'Your sins are forgiven you.' Forgiveness is a means of healing. It isn't simply the healing of relationships, though of course it can include that. In the healing of the sinner, or of the one who has caused offence, the one who offers forgiveness also benefits from the healing process, and often is healed as much as the person forgiven. Those who find it difficult or even impossible to forgive are burdened people. The heaviest load we can ever have to carry is a massive grudge.

Francis of Assisi, wrote, 'It is in giving that we receive, it is in pardoning that we are pardoned.' And 'It is in dying that we are born to eternal life.'

I think forgiveness is part of the essence of resurrection. I have seen people who were spiritually deadened by anger and hatred, people who spent years in a self-imposed limbo of bitterness, because of their inability to forgive someone. And I have seen the same people come to life through the healing power of forgiveness.

'Father, forgive them, they know not what they do.' That prayer was among the last words of Jesus Christ on the cross, and one of his last actions was the forgiveness and the promise of new life to the repentant thief. 'This day, you will be in Paradise with me.' That promise also revealed something of the nature of the forgiveness that is offered to those who turn to him. There is no waiting of any kind, no period of adjustment, no probationary period. 'This day – you will be in Paradise with me.' When God forgives, it is immediate; our sins are forgotten forever; we are made whole; and our restoration to wholeness, spiritual wholeness, is what the healing power of forgiveness achieves.

In the seventies, when I was broadcasting a series of meditations set to music, the response from the listeners was remarkable. The meditations stimulated hundreds of listeners to write to me about their difficulties and suffering. What became clear to me, after a time, was that the letters written to me were meditations in themselves. They were meditations on distress, yes, but I could see that they might have had a positive and therapeutic effect on the writer, in that by writing down the things that were troubling them, difficulties were isolated and identified and in effect reduced to their proper proportion.

Distress can distort things out of all proportion. People say, 'Oh, I've got so many problems I don't know where to begin.' Write them down, and 'so many problems' is reduced to two or three, or perhaps even one principal worry which is distorting our view of everything around us. Laying our troubles before God very frequently reduces them when we have to spell them out.

From my memory of the hundreds of letters I received from listeners, I think I could construct a letter that would not betray any individual but would give a fair representation of the general tenor of so many of the letters with regard to the corrosive effects of not being able to forgive. I think it would read something like this.

Dear Frank,
I think it is slowly becoming clear to me that I have never

fully understood what it means to forgive. Of course, I've gone through the motions. I've made apparently generous gestures; said, 'That's OK, don't worry about it', 'forget it', 'it's really all right', or I've said absolutely nothing. And it hasn't been all right because I didn't forget. Instead of letting the hurts out, I've held on to them, wilfully remembered them, nursed them, even rehearsed them in my head, and made internal, negative vows in a vain attempt to protect myself from ever being hurt in that way again.

Vows beginning with words like, 'That is the last time I will ever . . .' or 'from now on, I will never . . .' And all that my 'teeth-clenched' anger did was keep alive the hurt, or shut down and destroy some aspect of my own personality and life. The waste has been terrible: the waste of days, of years, of life, and we don't have enough life to waste. And the 'not forgiving', the 'not forgetting', the wilful remembering have been far more destructive than the original hurt. In retrospect, I can see that some of the 'hurts', though extremely painful to me, would be considered trivial to others, and because of that I've been unable to voice the pain, unable to say, 'That hurt!' And because I couldn't speak about it, I've nursed it inside, remembered these 'trivial' hurts for such a long time, and I've got such a good memory.

Well, I'd like to try – to attempt at least – a new method of dealing with those who have made me 'look back in anger'. Instead of gritting my teeth when a particular incident comes to mind I want, instead, to think of the person involved, and try to remember something good about them, in the hope that in the end, the bitter thoughts that have made me ill might be erased, by the power of the good.

Thank you for listening to all this.

Yours sincerely,

_____ _____

Inner healing is concerned with bringing to light the causes of the inner pain, to help the sufferer understand and interpret the causes correctly. This may well involve prayer and counselling rather more than having hands laid upon the person suffering. The book of Proverbs says that a merry heart does good like a medicine. It is also worth remembering that good humour and laughter and joy are spiritual, healing agents.

The Christian healer has to acknowledge that there are psychosomatic conditions and psychological disorders at the root of many physical illnesses. If a person with a healing gift can act as the catalyst between mental, physical and spiritual well-being, well and good, but a responsible healer will acquire enough training to make liaison with orthodox medicine not only possible but desirable.

So in meditation, in the ordering of our thoughts before God it is possible not only to discover that we have spiritual resources but we can also find both forgiveness and healing.

If 'meditation' is about ordering our thoughts, what then is contemplation? In Neville Ward's book, *The Use of Praying*, he says, 'There is a point in happiness, at which the mind simply "rests in enjoyment" and in happy tranquillity simply drinks in what is before it.' He goes on to give examples: 'The realisation that you love and are loved – sometimes defeats our attempts to find words to express our joy, and having no words there is nothing else to be done but silently rest in the centre of contentment.'

Other examples of 'resting in contentment' might occur when we listen to inspired music, or when a mist-covered landscape takes away our breath, or when sitting on a beach we become lost in watching the sea disperse in spray over rocks and sand. In such moments, we may be blessed by 'the peace which passes all understanding'.

Thomas Merton was a contemplative monk who, although he belonged to a silent order, still managed to make his voice heard by writing books, one of which was called,

Contemplation in a World of Action. He was aware that most people lived in a busy world, and that very few people appreciated the value of contemplative prayer. Most people feel they have not got time to be still and pray, let alone set aside hours for contemplation. In fact, some people feel that the prayerful lives of monks and nuns are wasted lives. They think that lives are only worthwhile if they're busy and active and 'doing things'!

Thomas Merton, however, argued that the real purpose of contemplation is to deepen one's love. He said that if you wanted to act and do things for the world, you should attempt to deepen your self-understanding and your capacity for love. If you haven't done this, he said, you will not have anything to give to others.

John Wesley was an extremely active man. He travelled thousands of miles on horseback, preached on village greens and in market squares, begged money from the rich and gave to the poor, wrote books, built preaching houses, and translated the French classics into English. However, this busy soul started every day by spending two hours in prayer, and during the day he fitted in a further couple of hours of prayer.

St Francis of Sales was another busy chap – he wrote books and was also the Bishop of Geneva. He said, 'Half an hour listening to God each day is essential; except when you're busy, then a full hour is necessary.' In other words, the busier we are, the more we need to practise being still in the presence of God. It is worth noticing that he did not say, 'Half an hour *talking* to God', but 'Half an hour *listening* to God'. An important ingredient of contemplative prayer is 'being still' in the presence of God, and in that stillness we give opportunity for the Holy Spirit to enter in, to heal and restore and equip us with the spiritual strength we need if we wish to serve our fellows with any real depth of love. It is good to begin to explore the peace that comes when we discover the meaning of being still in the presence of God.

Stuart Blanche said, 'Prayer is a relationship with God.' It is also an attempt to search out the mystery of divine love. It will, of course, take eternity to do that, so we all have a long way to go before we even begin to fathom the depths. But from my own very limited experience, I've come to know that if I can be still in my head, even for a few seconds, he will come into my mind, bring light when there is darkness, and replace anxiety with peace.

Once, I was in retreat at Aylesford Priory in Kent, with Rowanne Pascoe, a friend and colleague of many years. At that time, she was editor of the Catholic newspaper, the *Universe*. I wrote a prayer for her, called 'May Every Day'. This is it.

May every Day
Begin with space
Enough to see
My Saviour's face

May every hour
Possess within it
The space to live
A prayerful minute

And may I find
From night's alarms
The space between
My Saviour's arms.

A woman who went deeply into spiritual self-assessment was Teresa of Avila. For the instruction of the sisters in her order she began to write a book. To use her words, she had been 'begging the Lord to speak to me'. She wanted inspiration for her book and she was given a picture in her mind in which she saw the soul as resembling a castle formed out of a single diamond, or a very transparent crystal. Each facet of the crystal was a different 'room' in the castle and there were 'many rooms – or mansions'. Her book is called *The Interior Castle* or *The Mansions*.

She herself was very familiar with castles. It is thought that she was probably born in the castle at Avila. She lived in a period when most communities were built around and in castles. Some people lived outside the castle walls and only came inside when the community was under attack. Some people lived in the walls of the castle, others in the courtyards. The lord of the castle and his family lived in the inner chambers. In Teresa of Avila's *Interior Castle* there was, she said, in the midst of the interior castle a very special room reserved for God. The question she posed was, how do you enter this interior chamber? A slightly incongruous question, she suggested, because it was like asking, 'How do I enter a room I already occupy?' The door to this innermost chamber is prayer. This is the door through which we invite God to enter and make his home in our hearts, where we might sit and listen to him.

Being still and listening is a prayer skill that has to be practised. Most of us rarely stop talking. Even when we are apparently silent, we are still rehearsing things in our heads. Being still in the presence of God, or 'waiting on the Lord', requires us to say nothing, to ask nothing, but simply to accept that God knows what is in our hearts and minds; knows our needs, better than we do. If we could 'compose ourselves' – that is, in our breathing, let out, with every exhalation, all the stresses and strains and tensions of our lives, and with every inhalation, breathe in God's forgiveness and healing love – then our interior castle being filled with the love of God would mean that our capacity for love and for life would, with every breath, take us closer to the stature that was intended for us, which is, of course, the stature of Jesus Christ.

Your Sea is so Large and My Barque so Small

Some people have relationships with God which they find difficult to put into words. Women and men of action often express themselves more in the things they do than in the things they say but, every now and then, they reveal that the relationship they find difficult to describe is nonetheless profound.

When Sir Alec Rose was sailing around the world on his own, he found himself in the Southern Ocean with a desperate problem that required him getting to the top of the mast, in order to put a vital piece of equipment right. He later said that he could never have done it on his own, but as he went up the mast he became aware that he was not alone. He believes that God was with him in that situation.

Sir Robin Knox Johnson, who does not describe himself as a religious man, tells a story of when he was sailing in the Southern Ocean during his epic, non-stop solo circum-navigation of the world. He found, to his immense irritation that at just the time when he expected a following wind to drive him across the Southern Ocean, all the way to Australia, he was in fact faced with a very tedious and tiring headwind that went on day after day. He simply could not understand it. In these latitudes there was no landmass, nothing to stop the wind swirling around the bottom of the world in a clockwise direction, but here it was blowing full in his face from an anticlockwise direction, forcing him to lose time and to have to work very hard tacking against it. In total frustration at one point, he jumped up on his deck, shook his fist in anger at God, and shouted, 'God! Give me a bloody break, will you!'

He then went below, checked his chart yet again and found that he was not in the right place. He had made a navigational error. He altered course, and very shortly found the wind that he had been waiting for. In fact, it had been there all the time. It was just he and his yacht that were in the wrong place. It was as if God had heard his prayer and answered, saying, 'Don't blame me! Check your navigation again and I'll show you.'

Another round-the-world-solo sailor, who spoke of his relationship with God while he was at sea, was the Scottish sailor, Chay Blyth. When he was a guest on my television programme, I asked him, 'When you are alone at sea, does the loneliness get to you?'

'Well, it's really quite pleasant at times. All sorts of people can't get to you. You have a radio telephone but, unless you actually activate it and decide to call up, no one can communicate with you. So, you can't get the tax man after you. It's really quite pleasant, but of course you do get depressed at times, when things start to go wrong, especially after bad weather. You can get quite depressed.'

'Do you find yourself talking to yourself?'

'I don't think "talk" to yourself. You tend to give yourself instructions. You'll say, "The wind's dropping. You must get some more sail up" and you'll say, "Oh well, I'll wait a few more minutes." Then the other self will come in and say, "Come on. You're not here for a 'few more minutes', you know. So, let's get on with it." It's instruction rather than a discussion. We're quite normal, you know.'

'Do you have things that help, like music? Do you listen to music a lot?'

'I'm not too good with the old ear, but we do have music. I tend to celebrate things quite a lot. It seems to help the time go past. Burns Night, for example, and Old Years Night. Of course, you'd call it New Years Eve. We'd celebrate that, and we'd play music then, but generally speaking I don't bother too much.'

'Do you pray when you are on board?'

'Yes. I actually do pray. I feel quite guilty about it sometimes. I pray every single day we're at sea. Whether it's crossing the Channel, or going round Cape Horn. I pray every single day at sea. An extraordinary thing is that when we come back on land, I never go to church. I never pray. I get round that by saying to myself that he and I have got a deal together and that what we do is, he looks after me at sea, while on land I give him a plug.

'Well can you, by way of giving him a plug, remember any occasions when it seemed to you that prayer was answered at sea?'

'It's very difficult, because first of all it's a nice studio, it's nice and comfortable, and whenever you're in this situation, someone will come along and say, "Ah, that was all to do with the weather." There were a number of occasions when I would have a question mark, and think, "Was I helped out?"

'For example, the first time I attempted to sail round the world in a small boat that was totally unsuitable, water had got into my petrol, because it was kept in the keel. I could not generate and therefore I couldn't telephone back home and let my wife know I was OK. The result of that was that she was now faced with seven months waiting to find out whether I was alive or dead. And this was really most unfair and selfish. So I decided to call in to Tristan de Cunha in the Southern Ocean.

'A ship calls there only three times a year and, as luck would have it, the ship was there when I was there. Now you may say, "Well, that was just part of the thing. It was there, and that was that." But nevertheless, *three* times a year? *Exactly* when you want petrol?'

'Did you have to rendezvous with the ship?'

'When I sailed up to Tristan de Cunha, a full gale was blowing. It was pretty freaky, because it's all rocks and outcrops, but the gale sort of dropped, and I managed to get the petrol from the ship. I sailed off and, almost immediately, there was another gale. And as I say, you can tend to say, "Well, there was a front that had gone through", or whatever. But nevertheless, when you're on your own, you tend to say that fits the situation nice. You're OK. I'll give you another plug.'

'Are there particular prayers? Or do you just talk, as a human being talks, as it were?'

'Well, there again, you tend to be a bit selfish. It tends to relate to yourself. I have a little set thing, which I'm not going to say here, but we tend to have a little set thing and at the end of it you say, "If you've got time, you know, what about this problem I've got? You think you can help me out on it?"'

A moment with Chay Blyth that I will probably never forget came during the evening meal at the Queen's Hotel. We were discussing how, in a sophisticated world, belief in God was no longer considered very fashionable. Chay was sitting opposite me. He was smiling a kind of secret smile and there was a faraway look in his eye. Suddenly, the smile disappeared, and he looked up and said, 'Show me a man who doesn't believe in God, and let him come down with me to the Southern Ocean, and see if he's quite so cocky, down there.'

8 In Deserts, Gardens and Kitchens

Burning Sands and Cool, Clear Water

Being alone can change you. Most of us try to avoid being alone. If we do find ourselves alone, we will try to fill the silence with music, the radio or the television. In the New Testament, whenever Jesus made an important decision – about starting his ministry, or choosing disciples – he looked for solitude, either up a mountain or in the desert. People who either seek the isolation of lonely places or for whatever reason find themselves isolated from other people discover that in time they are changed by the experience.

June and I took *An Impossible God* to Maidstone in Kent. In fact, it was sitting in a cafe in Maidstone that I came up with an idea for a five-minute magazine programme, called *The Five Minute Show*. The idea was to incorporate as many elements as possible of a magazine programme into five minutes. Andrew Barr, who was then head of religious programmes for Southern Television, liked the idea. It was launched and ran for nearly two hundred programmes.

The eventual format for the programme included short introductions of the theme and of a guest. A caption asking a question would appear, followed by several, very quick, vox pop responses. I would begin to talk to the guest. Three out of every five guests were authors bringing out new books, which required a lot of reading on my part. A cartoon on the theme began to be drawn at the top of the programme, and a check on its progress occurred throughout the magazine. There was also linking music between the captions and the vox pops, very often strange and somewhat esoteric music using, for example, a Tibetan horn, bells and some very eccentric percussion.

The essence of the show was always the interview, but with music, captions, cartoon and vox pops it went along at a cracking pace. They ran for five night a week so, depending on the subject, sometimes the conversations would continue over two or even three nights. It was when I was making these programmes that I met Graham MacIntosh, who had given up his teaching job to spend nearly two years walking the parched and rugged coastline of Baja California, Mexico. He had written a book about his experiences called *Into a Desert Place*.

On a programme that lasts for only five minutes, it is essential that the interviewer should come straight to the point and ask very few, short questions. It is amazing how long people will continue speaking, if all you do is listen, and nod enthusiastically.

I asked him, 'Graham, why did you do it?'

'Two reasons really. First, I went out to that part of Mexico as a tourist and I just fell in love with the place. I saw all this cactus and rattlesnake, and scorpions. I went swimming in the sea and there were sharks and sting-rays and barracuda and I thought that this was a very special place. I fell in love with it. Most people hate it.'

I nodded encouragingly, and he continued. 'I came back to England and I was teaching unemployed youngsters at West Kent College. I found myself saying to them, "If you can't find work at the end of this course, why don't you consider getting a backpack, and going to France or see the world?" I couldn't believe how negative these young people were. They couldn't see that work is not the be-all and end-all of life. You could go off and have a great adventure and it needn't cost an arm and a leg, unless you get bitten by a shark, I suppose. I tried to persuade them to go, they wouldn't. Too negative, I suppose. So in the end, I talked myself into going, to prove a point.'

I nodded again. 'It's a very gratifying experience to have gone out there, and felt terrified and yet to have survived. The first week I would have gladly thrown the whole thing in. I got stuck in quicksand, which is a terrifying experience. I found I could hardly pick up my backpack. I was carrying 80 lb. It is 100 degrees, I'm a redhead, like yourself, and you can imagine being out in the sun. You blister. I had all these problems in the first week and it would have been so easy to have said, "I'm going home, forget it."'

I smiled. 'But I had said I was going to do this, publicly. I'd made a big issue of the fact that I was going out there and come what may I was going to do it. I stuck to my guns, saw it through.

'At the end of two years there was a great sense of "Yes, I have achieved something." Normally I'm the kind of person who is totally laid back, very fond of saying, "This is too much trouble. Forget it, let's go and do something else." But I had that goal, and come what may, I was going to see it through to the end, whatever the end might be.'

With my arms folded, one hand under my chin, I continued to look absorbed. I was. 'I know now that if I set a goal and really believe that I am going to pursue that goal to the very end, then I believe that I can surprise myself; whereas before, I had severe limitations. The chances are I couldn't, or wouldn't, do anything extraordinary. But having survived two years' walking, you get the feeling that maybe I should set more goals and try more things. I survived that. I managed to write a book. Who knows what else I am capable of?'

It was, I felt, time to speak. 'Graham,' I asked, 'what did you need to survive?'

'The most important problem in the desert, of course, is water, and I needed a variety of stills for making drinking water. Otherwise you need a lot of luck to survive. I was stung a couple of times by scorpions, and they can be deadly, so obviously if you are stung on the hand you have a much better chance than if you are stung on the neck. The most dangerous situation was probably dying of thirst. You need a gallon and a half a day. If you ration your water too strictly then you are going to be in trouble. Your system starts to collapse. That happened to me a few times, I could hardly stand up. I am struggling on my hands and knees to get down to the sea, partly to cool off, and so that I could use my stills. You haven't got time to worry about what's going to happen to you in that situation. If a rattlesnake strikes at you, it's over in ten seconds. It either bites you or it doesn't. But if you are dying of thirst, that can go on for several hours. You have time to think, "I wish I'd stayed back at home."'

'This must have built up your inner resources considerably,' I said.

'I suppose it did. I certainly found myself more spiritual at the end of the journey than at the beginning, less cynical. I was always very cynical about everything that smacked of religion. I didn't really understand. To me life was about DNA and the chemistry was all very clear. I couldn't see the need for the spiritual side, but the experience of being out there changed me totally. I felt so much that convinced me, that there was a hell of a lot more to life than there was before.'

'What was the most dangerous thing?'

'Lack of water. It is far more important than food. But there is something more important than water, according to all the survival books I read. The most important factor is morale. Once I had had that experience in the first couple of weeks I got quite depressed about it. I thought, "I can't handle this, I've bitten off more than I can chew." It's very easy in those circumstances to despair. You almost want to die; you think there's no way out of it. It's so terrifying that you can almost kill yourself because of your mental attitude. Once I'd got through that state I could see that the most important battle, throughout the rest of the trip, was the battle with morale, to believe that you are out there for a purpose, to believe that what you are doing is significant.'

I started the second programme with Graham MacIntosh by saying, 'The dictionary says that to survive is "to stay alive or to continue to exist". But there is a difference between merely existing and being truly alive. The will to survive only comes into operation when there's a reason for living. I suppose that's the eternal question, "What are we living for?" Graham, was the total isolation hard to bear?'

'At times, yes, particularly at the beginning. You go through a kind of culture shock where you leave the big city behind and you're suddenly out there. All the props and securities that you've known have been stripped away from you, you are there alone.

'I found that as the trip went on I enjoyed being alone. I found that if I was lonely, it was somebody else who had made me feel lonely. You might meet some tourists in the desert. They just can't believe this thing, walking up with a backpack, kettles banging and water bottles and the rest of it, maybe a rattlesnake in your hand as well. So they looked at you in a rather cold, hostile manner. Then you can feel lonely. But I could go back into the desert and spend another ten weeks on my own and I wouldn't feel lonely.'

'Why did you write a book? Wasn't the experience itself enough?'

'I think writing the book was an important factor in survival. I had to believe I was going to share this experience. Even if I didn't, I kept the journals and I was making tapes, because I felt that I wanted to believe it so much, to make the trip possible. Also, because I was teaching unemployed youngsters and because I had met so many people who were dissatisfied with their lives, I wanted to make the point that anybody can do this.'

'Was your loneliness eased by the fact that you were talking to a tape? Was that company for you, the tape and the diary?'

'I suppose so, because you always feel you are going to share it. So many beautiful things happened, as well as dangerous and exciting things. You do feel that you have to share it with someone. I always thought even if I get bitten by a rattlesnake or bitten in two by a shark, then at least there's a record of it.'

'Did the whole adventure bring out different aspects of personality that you didn't even know you had?'

'I was intrigued by this feeling that I had developed a sixth sense. I was psychic through being on my own. That really did intrigue me. I can remember times when something would happen and I knew it was going to happen. I had been thinking "scorpion" the day before I got stung by a scorpion. You think to yourself "Why?"

'I got away with so much I shouldn't have got away with, and I couldn't help wondering if that's because one of the greatest factors in survival is perhaps this sixth sense, which we don't use today in our lives.'

'You think most people have got it?'

'Perhaps we've got it and we don't take it seriously.'

'Oh, God, You Are Clever!'

People's spiritual experience of God is not confined to the rare and exotic, in oceans and deserts. June and I spent a wonderful evening with Dame Thora Hird. Over dinner at the Queen's Hotel, she told us about her adventurous life in the theatre and about her husband, Scottie, the love of her life. It is true that she has scaled great heights as an actress both in films and on stage and television, but as she talked to us she revealed that at heart and proud to be, she is a Lancashire lass from Morecambe, and her relationship with God is as much down to earth as it is 'spiritual'. She has been associated for many years with the television programme, *Songs of Praise*, and it became clear as we talked that prayer and praise were a natural part of her life, like breathing and laughing.

'Praise' in the ordinary sense of the word means an expression of admiration, but religious praise is much more than that. It involves all the ways in which it is possible to pay homage, or express our gratitude to God. We can offer our work, our days, our lives to God, as an act of praise, whatever we do, whether it's baking cakes or making people laugh. Mother Teresa of Calcutta said, 'I want to do something beautiful for God' and you could look at her life as an act of praise. Another life dedicated to God was John Wesley, the founder of Methodism, whose dying words, written down by those who had gathered around his bed, were quoted from the first verse of Isaac Watts' great hymn,

> *I'll praise my maker while I've breath;*
> *And when my voice is lost in death,*
> *Praise shall employ my nobler powers:*
> *My days of praise shall ne'er be past,*
> *While life and thought and being last,*
> *Or immortality endures.*

Religious praise is our response to the love of God. Some years ago I was in my friend Joan Martin's house in London, attempting to record for BBC Radio 4 an informal, intimate conversation with the song and hymnwriter, Sydney Carter. He was talking about his writing method when suddenly he leapt up and started dancing about the room singing and beating a biscuit tin, snatched from a table and held in the crook of his arm as if it were a small drum. He has spent his life writing songs and poetry, but he told me he couldn't compose songs simply in his head. He said he had to respond to his inspiration with his whole body. The result is frequently a very joyous response to God, perhaps never better expressed than in his 'Lord of the Dance' in which he sees the whole of life as a dance and the joyful leader of the dance being Jesus Christ himself.

When Thora Hird and I got into the television studio I asked her, 'Thora, what are your earliest memories of praising God?'

'Very early? I always said my prayers as a child, and went to Sunday school, went to chapel. I had five uncles who were all trawlermen, coming from Morecambe. I often used to hear people say to Uncle Robert, who had a beard and a 'gansey' (woollen sweater), "Ee! Robert, you do look like Jesus." Well, I thought that Jesus looked like him. So when I used to say "Gentle Jesus meek and mild", I never really understood it. I used to think of a man with a gansey on and who had arthritis, which was called rheumatism then.

'I used to say my prayers like everyone else. When you're a child, you think God can do all. I remember saying to God, "Bless my father, bless my mother and bless my brother Neville, and please bring me a nurse's uniform for Christmas, and don't let there be another war." I was only about five but they sold nurse uniforms on a piece of card and I thought God would bring me one. But this is all part of belief. If you think God can get you a nurse's uniform, you think God can do anything.'

'What sort of things make you want to praise God nowadays?'

She laughed. 'There wouldn't be time on ten of your programmes put together. I am so blessed as a person, because I have always been surrounded by so much love. Really, from the word go. A wonderful father, and a wonderful mother and brother, wonderful husband. Dear, darling, good daughter, two grandchildren, so what could I do, but be praising all the time for all these things?'

'I can understand that, as a response to all the love that surrounds you, but what about when things go wrong?'

'Like everyone else, when things go wrong, I say, "Oh dear, why has that happened to me?" I always find now, because I'm older, I just ask for a bit of extra strength to tolerate that, because if it didn't go wrong, we'd never enjoy the right bits, would we? Because he understands me. We have a wonderful relationship with that gentleman.'

'Do you speak as you do now, to the Almighty?'

'I do, and I've so much to thank him for I can tell you, and he's listening. Often my prayer is so long at night. Often I'll say, "Will you excuse me till morning?" And I'll finish it in the morning. The strange thing is that I've never woken up without finishing the prayer from the night before. Then I look out of the window and add something else, "Oh, you clever thing! What a lovely day it is." He's sick of me telling him about the flowers at our little cottage.'

'Do you praise God by literally looking at things and saying the words?'

'There's so much to praise him for, isn't there? I can come out of the cottage at half past five in the morning, "Oh, you clever thing! Look at the day, look at the birds, those flowers. How did you think to do all them? If you thought for ever, you can't think of all the blessings, can you? Well, I can't. If I was more educated perhaps I could, but for me, that's marvellous.'

'Working in the entertainment world, there's a lot of tragedy, a lot of unbelief, a lot of difficulties. Are the people that you work with affected by your attitude?'

'I'll just talk about *Hallelujah!* if I may, quickly. If I want to praise God, I'll say, "Thank you, Lord". This is why my character in *Hallelujah!*, Salvation Army Captain Emily Ridley, does this. So when I say any of those words, the people I work with know that is what I'd say in life, and I always mean it that way. I know this isn't the only way to praise him, but I've always been able to talk to him anyway. When we were first doing *In Loving Memory*, I had arthritis. I was limping about and in that dressing-room, and in that corridor, at the half-hour I used to pray. I used to take a little tablet as well, a pain-killer. I had the most wonderful arrangement with the Lord. I used to say, "Please, Lord, let me do the programme without limping and it doesn't matter how much pain I get when I get back to the hotel." Now he must have heard that because I went through that programme without a limp or anything, and when I got back to the hotel, I wish you could have seen me. I accepted that because I don't think there is anything God can't or won't do, an arrangement like that. Now I've got two tin hips, you see, I don't bother him very much.'

There's a passage in the book of Job, where the Lord says to Job, 'Where were you when I laid the foundation of the earth, when the morning stars sang together, and the sons of the morning shouted for joy?' To praise God is to show our gratitude by paying homage in words, music and most of all with our lives. When we are silenced by the beauty of the sky, uplifted by the freshness of the morning; when we are moved to help somebody; when we offer our services, smile at the sight of a friend; when we laugh, shout, clap our hands with joy, then we are expressing our gratitude to God. To respond to the beauty around us is as natural as breathing and whenever we do, whatever we call it, we're praising God.

Lord of the Pots and Pans

Delia Smith is, undoubtedly, one of British television's most popular and creative cooks. June and I first met her, one bright morning, at her home in East Anglia. We discussed what we might do on the television programme, and then I invited her to lunch. Taking a famous cook to lunch, as you might imagine, could easily be a somewhat daunting prospect. However, Delia is such a friendly and approachable person that I did not have any difficulty in sharing my dilemma with her. The problem was solved as soon as I told her that we had been booked into the Swan at Lavenham.

'Excellent,' she said. 'Let's have lunch there.'

I can't tell you the pleasure it gave me telephoning the hotel to ask if they could possibly reserve a quiet and reasonably private table for a lunch party with Delia Smith. On the other hand, I cannot begin to imagine the messages that must have passed between the hotel reception staff and the kitchen. Whatever those messages were, the lunch was excellent. One always imagines that famous cooks never eat anything that is less than exotic. Whereas in fact, fundamentally, their diets are not likely to be much different from anyone else's. It's just that they can usually think of that little 'something' that makes even the humblest dish a touch more interesting.

Delia Smith is known to television viewers as a cook. However, I was asked to review one of her books, which was not a book of recipes but a book of prayers and reflections, called *A Feast for Lent*. Since then she's written other spiritually reflective books. So when we met again in the television studio I asked her, 'Delia, how is it that a famous cook is now writing books of prayers and meditations?'

'Well,' she said, 'it came about quite unexpectedly, really. A producer rang me up one day and asked if she could come and make a programme about my faith. I had mentioned to a magazine journalist that I spent my spare time studying Scripture, so she said, "Can we just come along and make a programme about your faith?"

I said, "Yes". At the end of the programme the interviewer said, "Have you got any ambitions that you would like to do?" and I said I would like to write something spiritual. Having said that on the programme, one or two publishers contacted me and it grew from there.'

'In writing a book, how much do you feel that you are actually creating or being used within creation, as it were?'

'I actually feel that I am probably creating nothing but I think I'm being used. I feel very much, especially on the spiritual side, that it is a deep spiritual thing within, and that it is coming out in spite of me. I can read it through afterwards, at a much later time, and in a way learn something new myself. It's amazing, really.

'On the cookery side, again, there seems to be something within me that wants to communicate, that wants to share with others. It just seems to come out, in spite of me.'

'Do you actually set out to create a dish? Is that an exercise that you are used to?'

'Sometimes it's inspiration, and sometimes it's desperation, you know? You've really got to find something new, and you can be quite frantic thinking, "My goodness, is there another thing you can do with lambs' kidneys? I've done it all!" And then you sit down and think about it and suddenly an idea comes – the creation happens – you do think of something different.'

'I'm interested in the relationship between spirituality and food. How much are you aware of that kind of relationship in your cooking?'

'I think they are absolutely parallel. What I've learned, I think, through the work that I've done, is that if people are hungry for food to nourish them, it often turns out that they are hungry for spiritual food. The Scriptures are right, "Man does not live by bread alone, but by every word that proceeds from the mouth of God." Something that *really* feeds people will feed them both physically and spiritually. The physical and the spiritual are very close.'

'Brother Lawrence, who wrote *The Practice of the Presence of God*, once said, "In my kitchen, surrounded by all the noise of pots and pans and my brothers at work, I am as aware of the presence of God there as I am on my knees before the Blessed Sacrament." Do you ever feel that in your kitchen?'

'Oh, I do, yes. I think sometimes I get quite cross with God. I can spend a long time in prayer and hear nothing and then, in the middle of making a sauce or something, I get this feeling that God's speaking to me, and I think, why couldn't you have said that when I was with you in quiet? Yes, it's true. God is in everything, though, I couldn't sacrifice the quiet time. I feel as though I am only going to be aware of God in the rest of my life if I'm having the quiet time as well.'

'So you think you have to contribute to creating a spiritual dimension in your life? You have to do something about it?'

'Not *do* something, but be open to it, to respond. I feel that it isn't something you actually do. Often you seek and it's given to you. If you have a heart that's seeking God, yes, then you're receiving. Creation is happening within you, new life, new creation.'

'What about creation itself? Does that inspire you?'

'It does very much. I live in the country. I do try to go out and walk, quite a lot. When you're in prayer you sometimes feel that God is not there, you are in darkness, but when you can see a beautiful landscape, you've got a kind of image of him. You can look at a lovely sunset and say, "Gosh, I love you, Lord, you're beautiful." Because he is there, in his creation, and I find that gives me tremendous joy.'

'Would you say that prayer is the food that recreates you?'

'Definitely, because all God really asked us to do was love – love him, love our neighbour, love ourselves – and the only way this can happen is through a relationship. You can't love somebody you don't know and you can't know somebody you don't spend time with. I think that spending time in prayer is very important. As the psalmist said, "Be still and know that I am God."'

'Seeing God in creation is very understandable. Do you see God in suffering?'

'Yes. It's true there is an awareness of the presence of God in joy, but I think in suffering we realise we live in a fallen world. We realise our desperate need of God to overcome the pain of being human. I would say, yes, in suffering there's a deep awareness of God and our need for God.'

9 Agonising in Body, Mind and Spirit

Suffering: 'My God, My God, Why Have You Forsaken Me?'

Driving out of Leeds, I was thinking about the fact that we had two rather 'spaced out' engagements ahead of us. Not the best planning in the world – you try to avoid it but somehow every now and then it happens. Our first and immediate performance was to be in Stockport, Cheshire, and the next show was in Poole, Dorset. Then, with a little gap, after a short rest in Bristol, it was the Fringe season in Edinburgh. All our planning had been leading up to the Scottish enterprise. However, what was slowly dawning on both of us was that the preamble to the big adventure was proving as big an adventure as – the big adventure, if you see what I mean? In order to achieve the Edinburgh Festival Fringe we had accidentally created a way of life that seemed to suit us.

Out of the blue June said, 'You touched on a huge subject at the very last minute when you started talking to Delia Smith, about seeing God in suffering. Have you ever done a programme on suffering?'

'I once did a radio programme about three people who all reached different forms of breaking-point and whose spirituality enabled them to overcome the crisis they were facing.'

We were driving along the slip road leading on to the motorway. June signalled, a truck moved into the middle lane and we slipped into the world of the motorway.

'Have you ever made a programme that asks directly, "Why suffering?"'

'No, I don't think I have. It's an immensely difficult and complex subject. It's probably the subject which has caused more people to lose faith in God than any other.'

June glanced at the rear-view mirror, and then shortly after that I began to hear the police siren. In no time at all the orange and blue livery and the eye-aching strobe of the blue lights of two police cars streaked passed us at an incredible speed. 'One way or another,' I said, 'those lights probably mean that some poor soul is suffering somewhere on this motorway.'

June said, 'But you have met people who have suffered enormously and yet still hold on to their faith, haven't you?'

'Yes', I said. 'Probably the most memorable experience I ever had was shortly after leaving college. I think that experience put my own faith to the test, in my first week in practice as a minister.

'I had to visit a very sick woman in hospital. She was paralysed from the neck down. She had been in hospital for a very long time, over a year. I must confess that I was very worried about meeting her. She was going through a terrible ordeal. They probably have better ways of dealing with her condition now. I don't know. But in those days she lay in a plaster cast on her back for four hours, then a plaster cast was placed over her, secured with leather straps, and she was turned over and then spent the next four hours on her front. This went on continually, day and night, week after week and month after month.

'The more I thought about it, the more concerned I became about what comfort I could possibly offer her. What could I say to her? Even common small talk became more and more meaningless when I considered it. I wondered if I would even be able to say, "How are you?" Expressions like, "How do you feel?" were hardly appropriate in those particular circumstances. How cosy those pastoral theology discussions on "visiting the sick" seemed when I looked back on them. In plain words, I felt even more inadequate than I usually do as a minister.

'In the event, I did not comfort her, she comforted me. She took the initiative from the moment we met. She asked me about myself, my family, my college, the manse. She appeared to have an insatiable curiosity and a genuine interest in the new minister. She was so alive. She had a sparkle in her eye because of her wonderful sense of humour. She read a great deal when she was on her back. They had provided her with a frame on which a book could be placed and because she could move her head, she was able to turn the pages with a long stick, like a backscratcher, held between her teeth. When she was explaining this she made a joke about liking to "get her teeth into a good book".

'She told me that the previous Christmas she had sent a greetings card to every Methodist minister overseas. When I said, "That was very thoughtful of you", she laughed and said, "No, it wasn't. They nearly all wrote back. I received cards and letters from all over the world." She winked at me and said, "I collect foreign stamps. So, you see, I'm not so daft as I'm funny looking!" And she laughed again at the huge joke of it.'

June said, 'It can't have been easy keeping her spirits up. I simply can't imagine being able to survive under those circumstances. It must have been so incredibly frustrating. I am amazed that she didn't reach screaming pitch every day.'

'I know,' I said. 'It baffled me. Perhaps she did reach screaming pitch, but somehow diverted the scream into something else. There was no doubt about it, her courage was breathtaking. She told me about her prayers. She said, "I don't ask to be cured any more. I just ask for strength to get through the day." She seemed to know everyone in the hospital. No one passed by without her calling out to them. Just before I left, she said I would have to become a missionary and then I could send her a regular supply of foreign stamps. It almost seemed a good enough reason for going overseas.'

June said, 'How long did she survive like that?'

I said, 'I don't know. When we moved to another part of the country, she was still there and she seemed to be as strong on the day I left as she had been on the first day I met her. People were constantly trying to think of things that might improve the quality of her life. I suppose her condition was similar to that of the Superman film actor, Christopher Reeve. Now, he has an extraordinary spirit. It's almost as if suffering releases resources we did not know we had.

'The fact is, whenever I visited her, she did me good. When I left her, I felt buoyant, lifted up. She comforted me rather than the other way about. Leaving her was like stepping outside a magic circle. It was as if she was surrounded by an aura of happy vitality. I simply can't explain it.

'It was an extraordinary experience, but no clear, neat argument with regard to suffering formed in my head. No bright shaft of light brought lucid understanding to the awful inconsistencies and downright unfairness of suffering, but something clicked in my head, something made a kind of wild sense. I had the feeling that I was late in stepping into her arena, her battlefield, because she seemed to have won the battle already. I didn't really know what to think. She left me bewildered and elated at one and the same time.

'Suffering embitters and destroys some people. I know, I've seen it. With others, like this paraplegic woman, suffering is brought to heel. It may have imprisoned her body but it failed utterly to imprison her spirit. I doubt if I would ever be able to give an apologetic argument on the subject of suffering that would come within a stone's throw of that woman's testimony.'

June said, 'What do you think you learned from meeting her?'

I said, 'Well, of course, I cannot hope to understand fully the depth of her experience, but I think I learned more about faith in God and more about spiritual realities from listening and talking to her than from any argument I ever heard or read on the subject. I wish I had a mustard seed of her faith. When I hear the sophisticates of the world pouring scorn and derision on faith and dismissing religion as absurd, I think of the dignity and courage of that woman. Then a host of other courageous witnesses leap into my mind and it becomes immediately clear where I must take my stand, and it is certainly not alongside the cynic.'

June said, 'What did you mean when you said that you were comforted by her?'

I thought about the question for a moment, and then said, 'At the very beginning of Paul's second letter to the Corinthians, he talks about "the God of comfort, who comforts us, so that we may be able to comfort others". I think the word "comfort" has become something of a milksop word nowadays. It has lost a great deal of its original meaning. The literal meaning of "comfort" is "with strength". "Comfort" is a close relation of the word "fortify". So to "comfort" in the true sense does not mean "to sympathise", it means "to strengthen". So, I suppose I mean she gave me strength, to face my own doubts, my own fears. That's what I mean by being "comforted" by her.'

June said, 'It's not something that I find easy, visiting the sick, especially if they are critically ill, or severely handicapped, like the woman you visited.'

'It's difficult,' I said, 'to describe the trepidation one feels at the thought of visiting someone who is suffering greatly. To bring comfort to the suffering is one of the principal responsibilities of a minister. Those who believe they have been called to a pastoral ministry accept that it is a privilege, even if a formidable privilege, to be with people in all kinds of crises of mind and body, but nobody in their right mind would admit to it ever becoming any easier, no matter how many times they have shared desperate experiences with people.

'The difficulty for anyone who has had some theological training is that it is almost impossible to talk about suffering without at the same time considering providence, sin, creation, the nature of God, or for that matter the existence of God. But we can at least be honest and straightforward. For example, we can come to terms with the fact that, in the face of suffering – that is, in the presence of people in actual pain – a monologue on the Christian theology of suffering is not what is required. At that moment, people need their pain relieving in any practical way that it can be relieved, by pain-killers, or whatever. Then they need the encouragement and the security of our love, the promise of hope that our companionship gives. That is friendship that is going to stay with you when you need it. In these moments, what we are is far more important than anything we say.

'Having said that, we must accept that what we are depends on what we believe. And there *are* arguments – good, strong, rational arguments – that can help some people come to terms with suffering.'

June said, 'Just check with the map, would you? It is Exit 39, isn't it? For Denby Dale?'

We were making for Stockport and had thought that it might be pleasant to cut across through Denby Dale and then perhaps have a cup of tea in Holmfirth, the West Yorkshire location of the *Last of the Summer Wine* television series. I flicked to the appropriate page in the road map book.

'Yes, that's right. It's the A636 to Denby Dale and then the A365 to Holmfirth.'

'OK,' June said. 'So give me one.'

'One what?'

'An argument that might help me to come to terms with suffering.'

'Oh, yes, I see. Right.' I looked up from the map book in which I had been trying to find an interesting place to stop for a bite to eat on the way, and considered the question.

'People often say that they cannot believe in a loving God when there is so much suffering in the world, yet, paradoxically, a world without suffering might well be a world without love. I say "might" because it may be possible, for some, to know joy without pain, laughter without tears or to appreciate light without much knowledge of the dark.'

'Are you suggesting that no suffering means no love?'

'I think I am, yes. Almost anyway, certainly love of any depth or significance.'

June said, 'Perhaps you ought to spell that out a bit more.'

'Very well. I'll have a bash. When I was teaching I once asked a class of girls to imagine that they were God for a day, and to suggest ways in which they could improve on the world as it is at the moment. They came back saying that in their world there would be no suffering, no wickedness and everyone would love each other, which sounds fine, until you start looking at those ideas closely, and then you begin to see that they wouldn't really work.

'Take the idea of a world in which everybody loved each other. To love and be loved requires choice. We have to be able to choose to love, but if we lived in a world in which we had no choice about loving or not loving, then it would not really be love, would it? Love involves making difficult decisions, agonising choices. It involves passion and pain, but if everybody automatically loved everybody else, love as we know it, love of any depth or quality, would cease to exist.'

June nodded and extended the argument, saying, 'You could apply the same kind of argument to sin. If you had no choice about sin, if you were only capable of being "good", then your "good" or sinless actions would hardly have any value, because in order to be good, there has to be the possibility of not being good, or of choosing sin.'

'Precisely, my dear Watson. Now employ the same sort of argument to suffering. If there were no such thing as suffering, then there would never be a need for compassion.

The quality of compassion would simply cease to exist. So would the need to care, because with no suffering there would never be anyone in need of care.

'Now, put all these things together and ask yourself, "What sort of creatures would human beings be, if they were incapable of choosing to love, had no knowledge of doing good and no awareness or knowledge of the nature of compassion?" Whatever they were, they would be *lesser* beings than they are now. In fact, they would not be human. To be completely human, it seems, you need to have the possibility of suffering.

'Another point is that, very often, moral evil and suffering are treated as one problem. Some might be inclined to believe that all suffering and pain is evil. But it can't be as simple as that. For example, we might suffer from an uneasy conscience, but that is not necessarily a bad thing. The pain you feel if you put your hand too near a flame is a protective warning, telling you to take your hand away or it will be damaged.'

June was now signalling to leave the motorway in order to take the road for Denby Dale. She said, 'I suppose a "thrill" is a kind of enjoyable fear, and some people deliberately choose to do thrilling things, take risks in order to intensify their lives.'

'Yes. On the other hand, we also have to face the fact that suffering and pain, can be devastating and destructive. It isn't simply a question of how we view it. There are those who argue that suffering is not real, that it is all in the mind. Mary Baker Eddy, the founder of the Christian Science movement, taught that "mind" was the only reality and "matter" an illusion. Suffering and death, she said, are the effects of false thinking. The Christian Scientists are great advocates of the idea that there is nothing good or bad but thinking makes it so.

'The trouble is I *do* think, and thoughts are real, including evil thoughts. Why should I have them if they are not real? I also *think* I feel pain. There is a very good limerick on this. How does it go? Oh, yes.

> *There was a young lady in Deal*
> *Who said that pain wasn't real,*
> *But when I prick my skin*
> *With the end of a pin,*
> *I dislike what I fancy I feel.*

There is no getting away from it, suffering is a very complicated and puzzling subject. We can't say that good can come out of all suffering, even though the love of God for the world was revealed through the suffering of Jesus Christ. People are always trying to put forward arguments to save God's reputation in the matter of suffering. Unfortunately, like Mary Baker Eddy and the Christian Scientists, they produce rather weak theology.'

June said, 'Five miles to Holmfirth. What other arguments are there?'

We had joined the A635. I said, 'Another argument comes from those who say that good and evil are ultimate things, and because of this the devil is unavoidable. But this doesn't work in theological terms. There can only be one ultimate, one Creator. We can't have it both ways: one God and two creators, a good creator and a bad one. So we have to say that God created a world in which it was possible for loving creatures to exist, but to achieve that meant creating a world in which the opposite of love was also possible. To create creatures who have "free will" means that the possibility of disaster has to exist, even the possibility of evil, which is not the same as saying that God created evil. It is simply that for goodness to exist, evil has to be a possibility.'

June said, 'What about those who say that the human race is steadily improving and that we will eventually become less violent, less committed to fighting wars or, in other words, the human race is just slowly growing up?'

'Yes,' I said. 'That's the humanists' argument. It's a mildly attractive thought, but it is not borne out in history. The twentieth century is the worst possible century for arguing that the human race is slowly improving. We still kill and steal in the same way that our ancestors have done for thousands of years, except that we are more skilful at killing these days. We have now invented better, more sophisticated killing machines. In the First World War we killed millions in the trenches and battlefields of France. In the Second World War, six million Jews were murdered, and we've gone on creating killing fields ever since, from Vietnam to Bosnia. I don't think there is any evidence of human nature changing or improving.

'It also suggests the creation was the work of a bumbling amateur who didn't get it quite right, but might, one day. That's creating God in our own image, instead of the other way about. But scientists will tell you that the universe operates according to very strict and precise laws, which we break at our peril.

'The easiest way out is to say that there is no God, to take a fatalistic stance and say that you are either lucky or you are not. The problem of evil only arises then for the believer in God.'

June said, 'If you are a believer, even if you can't explain it, how do you live with the fact of suffering, particularly innocent suffering?'

I released my seat into a more upright position. I said, 'I think that we must accept that God knew what he was doing when he created the world as it is. Even though we may not understand fully, I think it is possible to "see through a glass darkly".'

June said, 'What things do we see "darkly"?'

'I think,' I said, 'we can see quite clearly those areas of suffering where evil, anger, hatred and envy can be held responsible for a great deal of the pain of the world. If by "evil" we mean "moral evil", then it is very clear that man has been, and no doubt will continue to be, very responsible. A huge amount of suffering, every day, is the direct result of moral evil. I don't need to give examples of suffering caused through greed, envy, lust for power or common-or-garden selfishness, though I could suggest that it is unreasonable to shake your fist at God if you have smoked forty cigarettes a day for thirty years and find yourself dying of lung cancer.

'Again, through the glass darkly, I think we can see that much suffering is the result of ignorance. Nature or the way the universe works is inexorable. You can't stop the tide; if you attempt it you will get very wet, or you may even drown. Volcanoes do not erupt at the whim of a temperamental God. They erupt because it is part of the process of material existence. Natural disasters do undoubtedly contribute to the world's sum of misery; and children and the innocent fall foul of ignorance and disease.

'So, seeing through the glass darkly we must ask, "Is ignorance evil? Is our ignorance of how to treat *disease* culpable ignorance?" If the human race spends its wealth on warfare and prestige at the expense of medical research, is our medical ignorance therefore a culpable ignorance, resulting in the unnecessary prolonging of suffering?

'We say we cannot blame ourselves for earthquakes, storms and floods but, on the other hand, the appalling landslides of mud that recently buried villages in Italy were said to be the result of irresponsible land exploitation and development. Dust bowls are frequently man-made; holes in the ionosphere are apparently created by pollution; and weather patterns are changing because of the burning down of forests. So we are not entirely innocents at the mercy of a capricious Mother Nature.

'I know some argue that when humans fell nature fell also, but I must confess that I find this meaningless. Fallen people may influence their habitat for better or for worse, but "nature", the material world, is inanimate. It cannot make moral judgments, good or bad, or wilfully change the nature of the universe for better or worse.'

June said, 'Lots of people believe that suffering is inflicted on them in some way. They say things like, "What have I done to deserve this?", as if their suffering was a punishment for past sins.'

'Yes,' I said, 'but that is largely superstition. People find it hard to accept the world as it is. The Bible says, "It rains on the just and the unjust". Virtue does not keep you dry, nor does it make you immune from disease, nor did it protect Jesus Christ from the agony of Gethsemane.'

June said, 'Whenever we hear about terrible disasters, it does give you a feeling of helplessness. The problems seem almost too big to tackle.'

'I know,' I said, 'but I think we have to try to do what we can. It reminds me of the story of the man who started to throw starfish, stranded on the beach, back into the sea. He was told that he was wasting his time, that it would make no difference because there were thousands of stranded starfish. He replied, as he threw yet another starfish back, "Well, it will make a difference to this one."'

June laughed. 'I like that story. I've heard you tell it before, but I like it.'

'Well, I think we have to try to fight moral evil, in the world and in ourselves. We ought to try to be involved in the battle to reduce unnecessary suffering, and we should at least protest as loudly as we can at the abuse of nature. At the same time, we have to accept that life is as it is, in the sense that it is inevitable that certain things will happen to us. We will all grow old. Our bodies will, in some cases, break down, wear out, cease to function. We will all face death but the Christian faith says that we don't have to face these things with mere stoicism.'

'What do you mean?' June asked.

'I don't know if I can put into words exactly what I mean. Whenever we face great suffering, it is likely that we will pray, like Our Lord in the Garden of Gethsemane, "Father, if it is possible, take this cup from me." Now, sometimes our problems are not as great as we thought, and perhaps our prayers are answered through all kinds of things – the balm of friendship, or medicine, or the great healer – time.

'Sometimes it seems as if our prayers are not answered, and our problem remains, and all we can do is go through it, or live with it. The answer to Christ's prayer was not the removal of his agony, but the revelation that he possessed the power not only to face what lay before him but also to triumph over the worst that people can do to people, the power to triumph over sin and death itself.

'I believe that when I was standing at the bedside of that paraplegic woman, her courage, and humour, her spirit, if you like, was almost tangible. It was as if I was standing within a special aura. I've thought about it a lot over the years, and I am now fairly convinced that when I was standing by her bed I was, in fact, standing in the presence of the power that took Christ through the crucifixion.

'It's an intriguing idea,' June said. 'But it doesn't explain or justify suffering.'

'You're right. There is no way to "explain" suffering, or the mind of the Creator when this astonishing world came into being. But whatever else you might say about it, it's certainly the best of all possible worlds for making saints. It reminds me of the conversation I had with Rev. Vernon Stone, who had been imprisoned in China when the Red Guard took over, and was kept in solitary confinement.

'In "solitary", he had come to terms with his position. He filled the lonely hours with prayer. In particular he meditated on the Passion and resurrection of Jesus. He asked himself, "What is the worst they can do? Kill me? My faith is in Jesus Christ who defeated sin and death, so killing me would achieve nothing. In fact, whatever they do they cannot separate me from the love of God poured out for me in the life, death and resurrection of Jesus Christ. I wonder if Paul's experiences of being beaten, stoned, arrested and imprisoned informed his thoughts when he wrote that wonderful passage in Romans 8: "I am convinced that neither death, nor life, nor angels, nor principalities, nor things present, nor things to come, nor powers, nor height, nor depth, nor any other creature, shall be able to separate us from the love of God, which is in Christ Jesus our Lord.'

'Every day, people cope with varying degrees of suffering. It's not a lot of comfort being told that there are people a lot worse off than you". A toothache can completely disable you. You cannot think of anything else. The world is revolving around the pain in your mouth. In the scale of "disasters", toothache may not rank very high but it doesn't help being told that. All suffering is relative. A broken toy can seem like the end of the world to a child because, for most children, the world does appear to revolve around them. They are not experienced enough for their pain to be eased by a larger view of the world. Nevertheless, you can argue that how we handle suffering at a very basic level is likely to be of great importance when more severe trials present themselves. Sometimes, the only way out of suffering is to look up and away from yourself and give yourself a feeling of respite by being involved in someone else's concerns. Sometimes sharing someone else's suffering helps ease your own pain.

'I was once involved in a television programme that asked, "Does suffering change people?" We started by putting the question to people in the street and were given some surprisingly mature answers, such as: "If there is one way in which you can mature quickly and strongly, it is through suffering" and "There are two types of people, basically. There is one whose experience of suffering makes them grow, and the other kind are those it tends to destroy."

'The guest on the programme was Diana Lamplugh. Diana Lamplugh's daughter, Susie, was an estate agent who went missing while taking a client to view a property, and has never been seen since. Diana Lamplugh set up a trust in

Susie's name. The motto of the trust is, 'From the end the beginning'.

I asked her, 'Diana, why did you choose those words?'

'What happened was that I was sitting in church, while we were at a conference. I was thinking, "What can we do to tell people what the trust means?" Then I saw, on the back of a bishop's cope, the signs for alpha and omega, and I thought they looked beautiful. I thought, "What do they mean?" They mean the beginning and the end, and I thought, "It is not the beginning and the end, it is the end of the beginning." I didn't even know about the Eliot poem then. It was as though, at that moment, Susie had been rubbed out, by a rubber; as though she had totally gone and it was the end. But it shouldn't be the end, otherwise that negated her life altogether. That's why we chose the motto.

'Nothing can make up for losing Susie. It is something that you cannot possibly make up for. You have to go through it, but good has definitely . . . I mean, without Susie disappearing, I don't think the Health and Safety Executive, for instance, would be having such a large conference on Violence in the Workplace.'

'Tell me about the trust.'

'You get a vast amount of energy when something happens to you like this . . . it's appalling. You get this tremendous energy and you want to do something about violence and aggression. You want, really, to go and look for her. We couldn't do that. We got in the way of the police.'

'Is the trust to help people combat aggression?'

'It's to help people to know different ways, learn different ways to diffuse it, avoid it, deal with it, and also to allow organisations to be able to set up training schemes. We've got another part of the trust that is helping the relatives and the friends of missing people. We have two aims.'

'What did setting up the trust do for you, personally?'

'It helped me realise, or some way work out, that her now definitely assumed death was not for nothing; that her life, in a way, is still lived; that her life was for some purpose.'

'Diana, what are the differences between someone going missing and someone dying?'

'It's completely different. I think that a lot of people don't realise that. Certainly the media don't. It's totally different. A lot of people thought I would be crying and wearing black, but you see, we didn't know that it was death, which it most likely was. But it took a long time to realise that there would not be news that "something unforeseen" had happened to her, or that she'd be waltzing back the next minute. You don't know how to react. You've got no idea, no guidelines, no perception of how you should behave. All you do, is to act how you feel, and the way you feel is to shout out loud, "Where are you?" '

'If somebody dies, you know exactly where you are, and there's a ritual, there's a rite of passage that you go through. But there's no rite of passage for those who are "missing", so what do you do?'

'It's very difficult. You don't know when to go back to work. Should you or shouldn't you go back to work? When should you, can you ever stop looking? If I was missing, wouldn't I expect people to go on looking? Even now, people say, is she out in a hot country, kept in a harem? Shouldn't you be out there? Well, should you? What do you do? If you haven't got any money, should you sell up, get out there?

'If someone's husband goes missing, you know, that is an appalling situation. I'm not saying someone they know has gone off with the secretary, or something like that, but if someone totally disappears one day, there are lots of different reasons why they could have gone off. They could have had burn-out, where people work to such an extent that they flip and don't even know who they are. Such a person deserves looking for.'

'Was there a point when you decided that you would have to behave as though Susie was not coming back?'

'Yes, of course, and the interesting thing was, looking back on it, that my husband reached that point at the same time. To start with, you don't want to tell each other, because you feel that you're letting your daughter down. You're letting each other down. The children were different, they reacted differently. We didn't understand that either. We had to learn to understand it. Susie is part of us. Susie is their sibling. That is a very different feeling, and the children wanted, literally, to get on with their lives. Susie was holding them back, and that was our fault. We weren't able to put her to one side and give them enough attention. This is something I had to learn.'

I once lost one of our children at the seaside, only for about five minutes, but during those five minutes I died a thousand deaths. I can't imagine how I would feel if one of my children was posted as officially missing. Diana Lamplugh has channelled much of her grief and pain into the Susie Lamplugh Trust. In order to give meaning to her daughter's life she focussed her energy on combating violence and aggression. She wrote a book called *Beating Aggression*, so I asked her, 'Why do you think people are aggressive?'

'There are a multitude of reasons. There is violence resulting from "chemical abuse", which is alcohol, drugs, glue-sniffing, that sort of thing. It can also occur when people are frustrated, they can't get their rights, they can't get a grant for their house, and so on.'

'An overreaction to injustice?'

'Well, perceived injustice. People can't communicate. They may want to make a point and somebody is not understanding that point. It is also to do with how you, physically, can raise aggression in other people by moving wrongly. People talk about someone "invading your territory". If you have your own office, or if you have your own space at home and you find somebody there, rifling through your things – maybe using your telephone, using your pad and pencil – you find yourself very much on the defensive. If somebody comes far too close to you, nose to nose, eyeball to eyeball, you find yourself backing away. You can also, quite inadvertently, raise aggression in other people with the wrong kind of voice.

'Fear makes you vulnerable. You are vulnerable when you are afraid, because you look like the kind of person who is what people call a "push-over", easy to attack. People attack people who are easy-going. Again, if you have an aeroplane constantly going over your house, your body reacts to it. If you are *constantly* meeting people who raise two fingers at you, who dig you in the ribs as they go by, at the end of the day you will snap.'

In the devotional part of my book, *An Impossible God*, at the tenth Station of the Cross which records the stripping of Christ's garments, I wrote a meditation on the vulnerability of love. Talking to Diana Lamplugh, and seeing her vulnerability and her suffering, and listening to her trying to understand what causes people to hurt each other, brought that meditation back to mind.

> *How vulnerable love is,*
> *how easy to attack.*
> *Yet somehow the stripping of Christ*
> *does not humiliate,*
> *doesn't reduce him.*
> *Rather, it increases our awareness*
> *of God's love*
> *for human frailty.*
>
> *In totalitarian regimes,*
> *whenever men attempt*
> *to reduce Christ,*
> *forbid him,*
> *with imprisonments and executions*
> *their efforts fail.*
> *In trying to suppress*
> *they only intensify his presence.*
> *Somehow*

*the stripped body of Christ
magnifies his love.*

Pulpits, Fonts and Communion Tables

If you spend an inordinate amount of time travelling up and down the country's motorways, quite early on in the process you find yourself making a list of dos and don'ts that make life bearable or unbearable. I'm talking about the basic necessities of life: eating, sleeping, having a shower. For instance, generally we try to avoid eating at motorway service stations.

We have been members of the National Trust for many years now and during the season – which is quite a long one, the bulk of the year, in fact – it's possible to find an interesting National Trust property which has a restaurant or café. We find the ambience of a National Trust house far more attractive than motorway service stations and the food is usually excellent. If there is time, we might have a quick look at the big house or abbey, or whatever it is. We constantly remind each other that this is all part of our working day and because we are working, the one thing we must not do is start enjoying ourselves wandering round great big houses. We work on the same principle as the advice that was given to certain Catholics at one time, with regard to whether or not they should indulge in sexual intercourse. The advice, when translated into plain language, apparently amounted to, 'Yes, you may, providing you don't enjoy it.' So we say to each other, 'Shall we look at the house?' and we might agree to do so, providing that we are quite certain we are not going to enjoy it.

One of the things we do enjoy is walking through the grounds of lovely houses. Many an idea has been pursued or wrestled with in the gardens of Dunham Massey or sitting outside the orangery at Kingston Lacey, or in the deer park at Tatton, or wandering around Vita Sackville-West's wonder-ful gardens at Sissinghurst Castle.

If there isn't an immediately convenient National Trust property for a midday meal, then sometimes we play pot luck by putting our finger on a village on the map, preferably just off the motorway, and as a result have discovered some lovely little country inns.

Having tea in the afternoon in England is something that you have to approach with a certain amount of caution because it can prove to be quite expensive. If you go to a place that is offering an 'all day breakfast' at a very reasonable price, you can often find that simply having a pot of tea and a toasted tea cake costs more than having an 'all day breakfast'. If you also have to stand and wait while a table is cleared before you are seated and if also you have to endure the Muzak choice of the company who own the chain of restaur-ants that you are patronising, then you very quickly decide that you might as well go to a hotel for your afternoon tea.

At first sight, you might think that this is an extravagant and expensive option, but if you go to the average country town, seek out a residential hotel as opposed to a pub, and go to the reception and ask if they are serving tea, you are usually shown into a very pleasant sitting-room. Tea is served in an agreeable environment and the personal service is lovely. I doubt if there is a great deal of difference in the cost at the end of the day and, even if there is, it seems worth it because at the end of that experience you are genuinely rested, you feel properly refreshed. As an added bonus note, loos usually have a much sweeter fragrance.

Another inexpensive and, to my mind, preferable alterna-tive to eating at a motorway service station is to take a picnic with you, so that you can get off the motorway, find a country lane, munch your roll and drink your coffee from the flask. It means that not only do you have a rural view but you can also see and hear the birds. June and I once met up with my 'father in God', Derrick Greeves and his wife, Nancy, in a field, off a lane that was an agreed halfway house, somewhere between Worcester and Bristol. Perhaps it was walking along that lane debating some esoteric issue with Derrick which began our habit of walking in green places and discussing work, life, family, theology and politics.

We had given our performance in Poole in Dorset on Saturday evening and on Sunday morning I had preached in the Methodist church. This particular church has what is possibly the largest pulpit in Methodism, and I have seen quite a few! It is made of marble and it reaches virtually from one side of the chapel to the other. Being in the pulpit was like being on the bridge of a ship. One of the church members who was a fisherman told me that their harvest festival placed a great deal of emphasis on the harvest of the sea. He said that the pulpit on Harvest Sunday was swathed with fishing nets and there was a green starboard light and a red port light on the appropriate sides of the pulpit.

By the end of this week we would be in Edinburgh for the Festival Fringe, but now we had time for a short breather in Bristol where our daughter Anne, our son-in-law Robert, and our grandchildren Suzannah and Julia live, and a few miles up the road from them, our son Mark and daughter-in-law Rachel are also within reach. After that we would be 'going over the top' for the big 'push' in Scotland. Today, however, we thought we might have a little visit to Kingston Lacy and take the risk of enjoying ourselves a little.

When we left Poole we had driven to Corfe Castle and then to Kingston Lacey, which is a National Trust house near Wimborne Minster. It was built to replace the family seat at Corfe Castle, which is now just a ruin. Kingston Lacey is set in a wooded park and there are lots of attractive, way-marked walks. The estate all around it is crossed by paths. You can actually get a leaflet from the shop which will help you to find a particular walk and the whole site is dominated by Badbury Rings, the Iron Age hill fort.

Walking in the grounds, June must have been ruminating

on Poole Methodist Church's massive pulpit, because she suddenly said, 'Why is it that so many Methodist chapels have a central pulpit?'

I gave it some thought and then said, 'The oldest Methodist buildings, of course, were not built as churches or chapels really, but as preaching-houses, and that is why the pulpit was, and in some places still is, so dominant. John Wesley would advise his hearers to go to church. The preaching-houses were simply for preaching and little else.

'The oldest Methodist buildings in the world, which are the "New Rooms" in Bristol, were built as accommodation for John Wesley and other travelling Methodist preachers and as a preaching-house. So the pulpit is central there and, of course, it's also the reason why, in most Methodist chapels, the font is usually a small, portable font, because in the original preaching-houses there were no fonts at all. Wesley expected Methodists to be baptised in the Church of England.'

I stopped, bent down to pick up an acorn and said, 'I think I'll put some of these in my pocket and see if I can grow a few oak trees, in pots, back home in the study.'

June said, 'Has Methodism always believed in infant baptism?'

'Yes,' I said. 'Initially, Methodist worship was an echo of Church of England worship and indeed Wesleyan Methodist services might have been quite difficult to distinguish from Church of England services, in content, but certainly baptism has always been a part of Methodism.'

June said, 'The Baptists don't actually believe in infant baptism, do they? What is it they call theirs? "Believer's baptism", isn't it?'

'Yes, that's right.'

'What's the difference?'

'Basically I suppose, the difference is that the Baptists believe that you have to make a conscious, intelligent decision to be baptised, whereas those who believe in "infant baptism" believe in what theologians call "prevenient grace", that is, grace that is given before we ask for it. In other words, we are loved by God whether we like it or not – it is part of God's nature, God's essence, to love. Divine love is spontaneous and its core is contained within itself. It is not dependent, in other words, on anything that we do.

'Baptism means a new existence, but it is not something that the believer can create or develop through their own efforts. It is given through God's grace. Actually from the earliest days of the Church, infant baptism was regarded as the norm. What infant baptism does is proclaim, with absolute clarity, that membership in the Church of Christ rests on nothing other than God's unearned, unmerited grace and love. Jesus once pointed to small children and said, "The kingdom of God belongs to such as these." Perhaps the great difference between a child and an adult is that the adult feels a need to earn the right to be loved, whereas the child simply accepts the love it is given, without any thought of having to "earn" or "deserve" it.

'Part of the problem in the debate about infant and believer's baptism lies, I think, in seeing baptism solely as an initiation rite. The Church is neither the total number of the baptised, nor the total number of the believers. The Church is Christ in union with the people belonging to him, the communion in which the Spirit is active. If you question the validity of infant baptism, you have to consider if this doesn't deny God's ability to give his grace to whomsoever he will. In other words, you make God's grace dependent on human qualifications. Instead of God's grace being freely given and received, you've introduced a kind of legalistic series of conditions which "allow" you to receive the grace of God. Those who believe in infant baptism believe that membership in the Church is not dependent on the examination or approval of any human being. No human judgment ought to be allowed to decide whether or not we belong to the Church of God.

'The whole of the gospel is about Jesus offering unmerited love to the entire human race, unearned. In Paul's letter to the Romans he says, "Christ died for the wicked." "It's a difficult thing," he said, "for someone to die for a righteous person; it may even be that someone might dare to die for a good person, but God has shown us how much he loves us in that while we were still sinners Christ died for us. We were God's enemies but he made us his friends through the love of his son."

'The difficulty with believer's baptism is that it excludes some people. It excludes the very young – indeed the very small children to whom, according to Jesus, the kingdom of God belongs. It excludes anybody who cannot express themselves or put into words their belief, their conviction about Jesus Christ. Baptism is about receiving grace. That's what we believe a sacrament does. It's a means of grace and grace comes only from God. To believe that we can only receive this grace when we go through a formula which requires intellectual understanding and assent makes the receiving of God's grace dependent not on God's generosity, but on human judgment. Let me give you an example of the difficulties created.

'I once had a friend call on me who belonged to a church which believed and practised believer's baptism. This person was troubled because every week people came to their church from a local home. Some of these people had severe learning difficulties. Because of this they were not able to read or write, and they would certainly find it very difficult to grasp theological ideas or religious argument.

'One of these people from this home, who had particularly severe learning difficulties, came to church and asked to be baptised. My friend's difficulty was in knowing how to respond to this request, because this person would not be able to fill in the form which was required and in which they confessed their belief in the saving grace of Jesus. Not only was he not able to understand the questions and fill in the form, but he wasn't even capable of signing his own name. We have to ask, is such a person to be excluded from baptism, and excluded from the grace that is available in the sacrament because they can't qualify according to certain human conditions?'

June asked, 'How did you advise your friend?'

'There's a little rule I use when I have a difficult decision to make. It's this: "When in doubt, do the most loving thing." And usually the most loving thing is the right thing to do. It doesn't mean that the most loving thing is always the easiest thing to do, sometimes the most loving thing is hard. I advised, in this particular case, that the form be filled in for this person and a blind eye be turned to his inability to read and write and fill in forms. What they actually did in the end I don't know.

'Infant baptism is not a magical rite. I do not think that if you go through the motions and do the right things that the full benefit of being baptised is automatically realised. It ought never to happen in isolation. A child being baptised ought to be baptised within an environment of faith, within a community where faith can be fed and nurtured and enable that child to grow in Christian maturity.'

We reached the car park and climbed into the car. Kingston Lacey is about a mile and a half to the west of Wimborne Minster.

June said, 'Blandford Forum, Warminster, Bath, Bristol?'

'Sounds good to me,' I said.

'What about Holy Communion,' she said. 'What are the main arguments about that?'

'I suppose you could say that it all revolves around the question of the "real presence", or you might in some cases talk about the "real absence". The Roman Catholics have a doctrine of the Eucharist called "transubstantiation". It was defined in the thirteenth century, but it is based on an Aristotelian philosophy about accidents and substance. The argument is that certain things might have the appearance of one thing but the substance of something else. For example, the "accident" of wood might in reality have the "substance" of something else, as when a veneer gives the outward appearance of wood while hiding an inner substance which is in fact not wood. This idea of accidents and substance was applied to an understanding of what happens at Holy Communion, that at the words of consecration there is a physical change in the elements of bread and wine. While they maintain the accident, that is the appearance, of bread and wine, the substance changes and becomes the actual flesh and blood of Jesus Christ. That's transubstantiation.

'At the Reformation, Martin Luther introduced the idea of "consubstantiation". This understanding of the Eucharist says that the bread and the wine are not changed, but the presence of Christ is nevertheless real. Martin Luther thought that the doctrine of transubstantiation was an absurdity, an attempt to rationalise a spiritual mystery. For Luther, the crucial point was that Christ was really present at the Eucharist and theories as to how that came about were secondary. The fact of Christ's presence at the Eucharist was more important than any theory or explanation.

'A third understanding of the Eucharist could be called "memorialism" or the doctrine of the "real absence". This idea is, I think, associated with a man called Zwingli, Huldrych Zwingli. To him there was no mystery to be explained, either by transubstantiation or consubstantiation. As far as he was concerned the whole Eucharistic rite was a memorial. Zwingli argued that you could not take the words, "This is my body" literally. He said that there were innumerable passages in Scripture where the word "is" means "signifies". In which case, "This is my body" simply means, "This signifies my body."

'In the New Testament, Paul points out that the Lord's Supper is always connected with death on the cross: 'For as often as you eat this bread and drink the cup you proclaim the Lord's death until he comes." John is concerned about the same idea, he keeps referring to "the word becoming flesh". According to John, the presence of Christ in the Lord's Supper is the presence of the living, life-giving Lord and Spirit. Christ is none other than he who has come in the flesh. So for John, the presence of Christ in the Lord's Supper is as real as his presence with the disciples during his days of earthly ministry, and it is the resurrected Christ who joins us all in communion round the table.

'The promise Jesus made was primarily about communion with himself, and if that is what he promised it must be much more than mere memorialism, mere symbolism. The words of institution leave little room for doubt that the Eucharist is entirely to do with his real presence, his communion with us and our communion with him, and through him, our communion with the whole Church, which is the body of Christ.

'There is a lovely word picture of what happens at the Lord's Supper, which says that when we gather around our communion table we are, as it were, holding hands with Jesus, and, at the same time, holding hands with our neighbours, who in turn are holding hands in a consecutive line, back down through the generations until we are linked hand in hand with the apostles sitting around the last supper table.'

Bagpipe, Kilt and Sporran

Suddenly we were there, in Edinburgh. Andrew 'Augie' Wright, a school-friend of our son Simon, had generously offered us the use of his apartment. Not that it was vacant or unoccupied in any way. His generosity was royal. He gave up his own bedroom, but no sooner had we arrived than the room filled up not only with our family, Anne and Mark, sleeping in sleeping bags on the floor, but also their friends. Getting out of bed in the middle of the night presented an indescribable obstacle course. However, when all were safely gathered in we could at least close the door on those who were sleeping in the corridor or carousing around the electric organ in the living-room. There was a Bohemian gaiety and wildness about the people who came and went, frequently through the living-room window, though the later the hour the more Dostoyevskyan and Russian the carousing at the organ became.

Edinburgh becomes truly festive throughout its Festival season with official and unofficial events happening in every available space, from shop doorways and pavements to theatres, parks and concert halls. I can understand why some locals abandon the city for the duration of the Festival. It's impossible to walk down Princes Street without being showered with leaflets and invitations to visit this, that or the other show or event. There are people on stilts, in clown costumes, dancing, singing and playing musical instruments. With over a thousand shows opening up on the first night the streets are alive with actors, singers, dancers and performers of every description. Billboards, shop windows and lampposts are hung with posters advertising this show or the next.

The ideal setting for *An Impossible God* is a stone-pillared church. There is only one such church in Princes Street, and we were in it. Because the church was host to a wide selection of events at different times during the day, they had their own publicity system, which meant that in addition to our own publicity we were also being advertised by the church's festival promoters. It undoubtedly made a considerable difference to the numbers who attended. In addition, logistically speaking, we were ideally placed for the office worker wanting to snatch a lunch-time performance.

One of the difficulties of doing two performances a day at two different venues was that we had to set up and take down our lighting and sound equipment and then move to the other building and set it up and take it down again, for each performance. That was a lot of rigging and derigging, and humping in and out of vehicles. At first there appeared to be a problem about getting into the Princes Street church in time to set up for the 12.30 p.m. performance.

We needed to start unloading the equipment every morning just before 10 a.m. At exactly the same time every morning, a military band of regimental army pipers, in full highland regalia – kilts, sporrans, tartan plaids and bagpipes skirling – marched around the corner from Princes Street and past the west door of the church in Lothian Road on their way to the castle. They were preceded a few minutes earlier by policemen who cleared the way, and parking outside the west door of the church even to unload became out of the question at that time.

On the first morning we were just finishing our unloading, completely unaware that in a few minutes we would find ourselves in the path of the unstoppable pipers. The police advance clearing party arrived and told us in very plain language that we had to move within the next two minutes. We did, asking as we left, 'How often do the pipers march past here?'

The reply was simple and direct, 'Every day, at *exactly* the same time.'

We moved up our schedule by five minutes and every morning exchanged greetings with the police as they arrived and we left. As we clearly operated with the same clockwork precision as the pipers, our relationship with the policemen became one of quite friendly familiarity.

During the first week, the daily paper, the *Scotsman*, sent a reviewer to each of our three shows. All the reviews were favourable and gave us their seal of approval. This was immensely important to us and probably set in motion most of the good things that followed, as far as publicity was concerned.

The first good thing was an invitation from Brian Matthews to appear on his BBC Radio 2 show, *Around Midnight* which was broadcast nationally, from Edinburgh, every night throughout the Festival. The producer was setting up a special programme with Brian talking to actors presenting one-man or one-woman shows. As I was the only actor performing *three* one-man shows, that fact, together with the three good reviews, undoubtedly secured my place in his 'one-man' special.

Then, my old friend and colleague from the BBC in Scotland, Douglas Aitkin, asked me to prepare a programme with him, to go out on BBC Scotland's Radio 4 in the Sunday morning religious programme on the first Sunday of the Festival. I was delighted. I was even more delighted when the programme planning meeting ended up with the decision to devote the entire forty-five minutes of the programme to discussion about and extracts from *An Impossible God*. Also, in that first week there was an interview broadcast about all three productions on the independent commercial radio station, Forth FM.

It was almost unbelievable. All the hard work and preparation had produced wonderful results: the *Scotsman* reviews and three broadcasts. We could not have hoped for more.

The daily routine, in addition to the double setting-up of lighting, sound equipment and sets, also involved some of us selling tickets at the door for the Nicolson Square performances. All of this, although exciting and a great deal of fun, was very demanding and physically very tiring, though one positive aspect of this, undoubtedly, was the fact that we were so tired that no matter what excesses were achieved by the organ-playing Brothers Karamazov, we slept through it all.

If you are doing two shows a day it makes it very difficult to see other performers at work. We did manage to catch a couple of shows and June went out, late at night, to see the fireworks display. There is a performers club at the Fringe headquarters which is based in the university, and a late night 'ad hoc' cabaret, which gives performers an opportunity to catch up with what their colleagues are doing. You can also eat there fairly cheaply, or perhaps it was especially cheap the night we ate there when the main dish offered was – haggis and swede. An acquired taste, I think.

Initially I was a little nervous about performing a play like *Steinbeck: Dispatches* with such a variety of American dialects in a festival which was clearly high on the American Scottish tour itinerary. I needn't have worried. The United States is a very big country and a lot of its inhabitants have become familiar with the more subtle nuances of American dialect in the same way I have, through the movies. Perhaps, another contributory factor might also be the fact that all the Americans I met were extremely polite.

Well, we did it, and we are alive, well and kicking. In the process we have laughed a lot, cried a bit, and learned a great deal about the motorways, A-roads, B-roads, and unclassified roads of England, Wales and Scotland. We have even learned a bit more about each other, even when we thought that was hardly possible.

Footnote

'We've been together now for forty years.' We have. It goes without saying that there are many ideas that defeat my ability to express them in words, but among the most impossible must be my thoughts about June, about our friendship and commitment, companionship and teamwork over so many years. I need to invoke St Paul's 'groans too deep for words'. The romantic concepts summoned immediately by the word 'love' seem to me to be inadequate somehow, seem to lack the vigour needed. They are not tough enough, not strong enough. It would need, I think, a wild and irregular poetry that could interweave harmony and conflict in the same breath, could wrap itself around the paradoxical; things like inexpressible joy, anger, pain, excitement, parenthood, passion, frustration, success, tear-stained laughter, adventure and wanderlust, hopes, dreams and crushing disappointment. It would need to weld together depression and courage, eyeball-to-eyeball delight and toe-to-toe confrontation. It would need to perceive the independent spirit that holds each other up in arm-in-arm dependency, and also allow that although they look, just conceivably, as if they might be on the verge of a pension, they clearly have no understanding of retirement, not as long as there are seas to sail or mountains to climb.

Yes. Well. I just felt I wanted to say that, or something like it.

'Where did you say we were going next?'

'Egremont. The Agricultural Halls, Egremont, Cumbria.'

'And then?'

'The Civic Theatre, Barrow in Furness.'

'And then?'

'The Methodist Church, Cockermouth.'

'Hmm.'

The car that has carried us and our equipment around the country over the last four years is a Volvo 760 Turbo Estate. The springing has been reinforced because of the equipment weight, but otherwise it is the same body, automatic gearbox and engine. The milometer is now reading somewhere in the region of a quarter of a million miles.

Anyone want to buy an old banger?